Your Encounters *The* *with* Holy Spirit

Name and Share Them—Seek More

DAVID S. LUECKE

WESTBOW·
PRESS
A DIVISION OF THOMAS NELSON
& ZONDERVAN

Scripture taken from the Holy Bible, NEW INTERNATIONAL VERSION®. Copyright © 1973, 1978, 1984 by Biblica, Inc. All rights reserved worldwide. Used by permission. NEW INTERNATIONAL VERSION® and NIV® are registered trademarks of Biblica, Inc. Use of either trademark for the offering of goods or services requires the prior written consent of Biblica US, Inc.

WestBow Press books may be ordered through booksellers or by contacting:

WestBow Press
A Division of Thomas Nelson & Zondervan
1663 Liberty Drive
Bloomington, IN 47403
www.westbowpress.com
1 (866) 928-1240

ISBN: 978-1-4908-3008-7 (sc)
ISBN: 978-1-4908-3009-4 (hc)
ISBN: 978-1-4908-3007-0 (e)

Library of Congress Control Number: 2014905410

Printed in the United States of America.

WestBow Press rev. date: 3/26/2014

CONTENTS

PART I
The Benefits of Recognizing the Spirit at Work

CHAPTER 1
Why The Holy Spirit Is So Important Today

If fathers know how to give good gifts to their
children, how much more will your heavenly Father
give the Holy Spirit to those who ask him!
—LUKE 11:13 (NIV)

The question is simple: what has the Holy Spirit done in your life lately? Yet it can bring different responses from equally sincere Christians. Some have a ready answer. The rest of us would have to think a while. We are not used to the question and thus struggle with an answer. The Spirit brought me into saving faith. True. But what about lately, say, in the last month or two?

Most of us Christians in America find ourselves in a centuries-old church heritage that places a strong emphasis on what God the Father and his Son Jesus Christ did in biblical times. But being spirit, the Holy Spirit is harder to envision than a father and a son, especially when in older English he was the Holy *Ghost*, of all things. Too often we gain the impression that the Spirit was some kind of vague ghostly presence, only in biblical times.

Why should a Mary Anne or a Mike or anyone else sitting in the pew of a Presbyterian, Lutheran, or Baptist congregation care what the Holy Spirit has done in his or her life lately? Better yet, why should their pastor try to teach them what to look for?

The goal of this book is to help believers recognize and more actively seek what the Spirit can bring now. When they know what they are looking for, I firmly believe that the Mary Annes and Mikes and other ordinary Christians in traditional church bodies will discover more excitement and fulfillment in their personal spiritual lives. Pastors who learn how to teach them will find that their congregation is becoming spiritually more exciting. Let the focus be on the "normal" gifts of the Spirit, highly prized in any congregation.

Sometimes the Spirit makes himself obvious, as in a personal awakening to a new awareness of God's love and greater motivation for Christlike living. Recognize the Spirit at work also in a fresh insight into how to apply the gospel to a difficult personal relationship or in readiness to take a new, seemingly risky step in trust that God will provide. Look for the Holy Spirit touching a believer's human spirit and bringing unusual times of abundant joy, peace and patience. Learn to spot what the apostle Paul calls the ministry gifts of the Spirit and the fruit of the Spirit in action.

NAME, SHARE, AND SEEK ENCOUNTERS

All Christians have encountered the Spirit. The apostle Paul explains, "No one can say 'Jesus Christ is Lord' except by the Holy Spirit" (1 Corinthians 12:3 NIV). All who confess the Apostles' Creed declare their belief in the third person of the Trinity, the Holy Spirit.

Yet most Christians expect little of the Spirit today, especially those of us in mainline traditional church bodies. We tend to leave the Spirit back in those days when Jesus and Paul said so much about him. We are too easily satisfied to keep the Holy Spirit confined to the creeds. While we confess Trinitarian beliefs about Father, Son, and Holy Spirit, we practice binitarian ministry, emphasizing the Father and the Son but for the most part forgetting the Spirit.

That is too bad. Our lives will be spiritually richer:

- ✓ when we learn how to *recognize* encounters with the Spirit in our lives today,
- ✓ when we *share* these Spirit encounters with others, and then
- ✓ when we deliberately *seek more* of the Spirit's influence in the days ahead.

We are used to thinking about objective truth—the kind we confess in creeds and catechisms. These doctrines about God the Father and God the Son, about human sin and the gospel are very important and set the context for the Father's and the Son's advocate, the Holy Spirit, the third person of the Trinity. Always within the context of God's Word, the Spirit's job is to turn these objective truths into what is true for an individual believer. Such subjective truth amounts to the life-changing relationship of trust in Christ, who acted on our behalf. Such trust happens when the Holy Spirit comes to each personally as God's grace in action.

"Having a personal relationship with Christ" is a good phrase heard among some Christians. It is implied in the Reformers' theology of "Christ for me" but is not much highlighted in my experience.

Name an encounter when it happens. *Share* these encounters with others, when and where appropriate. *Seek* more encounters by preparing yourself and inviting the Spirit. These pursuits will provide an improved rhythm for living the abundant life that Jesus came to provide for his followers (John 10:10).

Such rhythm can amount to modifying a church culture, which is made up of a congregation's beliefs, values, and behaviors passed on to others. Greater emphasis on the Spirit does not need to change *beliefs* about the Father and the Son; rather, it adds better understanding of what they do for us today through their Advocate, the Holy Spirit. Let a church's *values* be modified to highlight *behaviors* that name and share recent encounters with the Holy Spirit and then the behaviors to seek more.

Presbyterian pastor and psychologist J. Harold Ellens notes that experiences of God are common in our lives, when we know beyond a shadow of doubt that they are of God. Too often, we rationalize them away. He thinks this happens because we do not name and share them, thus including them in a conscious culture of the Holy Spirit. "For our best growth in the spirit, it is imperative that we name, share, remember and cultivate them, so we may be a celebrating people of God." He goes on to explain,

> The reign of God is present where we are living by and with the spirit of God in our spirits. Our moments of the spirit are those occasions when something develops in life that graphically or subtly illustrates that love works and grace heals. It is important to name those moments and tell others about them, so we become a people of the spirit, cultivating a culture of the Holy Spirit.[1]

Ellens offers the phrase "sailing close to the wind." A nautical term, it describes one of the most exciting experiences of sailing a boat. Sailing close to the wind puts the craft on the edge of being blown over. It then has to be counterbalanced, with sailors leaning over the opposite side. Keeping the sail set close to the wind offers speed and excitement. But it takes experience to lessen the risk. It also depends on team work.

The Holy Spirit is God's wind in our lives today. He can bring excitement to believers on their journey to becoming more like Christ. But we need experience and team work to reliably recognize the Spirit's leading. When in faith we do take risks and sail close to the Spirit-wind, our personal and church lives will be far from boring.

THE FATHER WANTS US TO ASK FOR HIS SPIRIT

The invitation to ask for the Spirit is found in that very familiar passage of Jesus' teaching on prayer. "Ask and it will be given to you; seek and you will find; knock and the door will be opened to you. For everyone who asks receives; he who seeks finds; and to him who knocks, the door will be opened" (Luke 11: 9–10). It does not take long for Christians to figure out that this promise does not extend to anything and everything we might want. For that, he reserves the right to say no or later.

What Jesus is really talking about, however, comes two verses later. If fathers know how to give good gifts to their children, "how much more will your Father in heaven give the Holy Spirit to those who ask him!" (Luke 11:13).

God is quite capable of sending his Spirit without our asking or knocking. He does this when dispatching his Spirit to bring someone to faith and at times to initiate spiritual growth spurts. So why does God expect us to ask for the Spirit, whom he promises always to send? My answer is that he wants us to ask for specific movements of the Spirit among specific people. He wants us to form clear expectations so that we can observe when, in fact, the Spirit has moved. We are more likely to see what we expect than to notice something we are not looking for.

T. M. Luhrmann is professor of anthropology at Stanford University. She was a participant observer and researcher in two different Vineyard Christian Fellowships over a number of years around 2000. She concludes that

> Coming to a committed belief in God was more like learning *to do* something than *to think* something. I would describe what I saw as a theory of attentional learning—the way you pay attention determines your experience of God.[2]

Just as anthropologists are trained to see what others miss, so Christians can be trained to see what many other Christians miss.

Luhrmann concludes,

> So churches like the Vineyard teach congregants to find God in their minds and to discern which thoughts, images and sensations might be God's word. The congregants practice having minds that are not private but open to the experience of an external God. These faith practices change people.[3]

Luhrmann also observes, "Whether those were authentic experiences of God cannot be determined by an 'outside' observer. That is why being in a faith community is so important."[4]

While her language is different, Luhrmann's descriptions fit within the classical Christian literature on spiritual development.

As Jesus explained to his disciples, When I go away, I will send the Advocate, the Holy Spirit, to you. "He will take from what is mine and make it known to you" (John 16: 7, 15).

MOTIVATED BY THE SPIRIT

Luke recounts that just before Jesus ascended into heaven, he told his disciples that he was going to send what the Father promised, and so, "Stay in the city until you have been clothed with power from on high" (Luke 24:49). This is special power, different from what is humanly available among us below. The focus of this book will be on understanding and getting ready for what Paul calls the gifts of the Spirit and a subcategory of fruit of the Spirit. These are the special powers of the Spirit to energize God's people in special ways.

Human motivation, for ordinary people, is something I know as a psychologist and former graduate professor of organizational behavior. The classic framework for understanding the personal needs people are driven to fill was offered by Abraham Maslow. It remains popular because it intuitively makes sense. Primary are meeting bodily needs like hunger, followed by the drive to find predictable security. At a higher level are the needs for affiliation and status. The highest, according to Maslow, is self-actualization.

Dominant needs shifted upward over the twentieth century. Security was very important and provided motivation to workers in the early years of that century and then affiliation. Status needs took on more importance in the latter part of the twentieth century. In recent times of economic uncertainty, motivational needs shifted back downward to a higher drive for the security of employer benefits, like health insurance.

Churches have been proficient at appealing to the range of human needs. Think medical missions in underdeveloped countries. Recognize the security offered by unchanging traditions and fortress-like church buildings in the inner city. In the first half of the twentieth century, there was a clear status ranking among Protestant churches. At the top was Episcopalian, followed by Presbyterian. At the bottom were ethnic churches and Pentecostals. Many Christians were driven to changed membership as they moved up socially.

The drive for affiliation with others became dominant in the 1950s and 1960s, with the out-migration from the cities to the suburbs. Most church bodies successfully planted many congregations, when "joining" all sorts of social organizations was a strong drive. Such motivation is now disappearing, as documented by Harvard sociologist Robert Putnam in his report in *Bowling Alone*.[5] He observes that while bowling is now more popular than ever, the number of bowlers who join teams in organized leagues is plummeting. Such a diminished affiliation drive is affecting lodges, veteran organizations, and also churches across the board. The key question for churches now is how to adapt.

Surely the Holy Spirit was at work among Christians that developed church emphases addressed to human motivations that were dominant in these differing social and economic circumstances. Wherever Christians are gathered in the name of Christ, there is the Holy Spirit. But the cultural context for younger generations today is different from the context churches successfully addressed in earlier times of dominant needs for security, status, and affiliation.

Christian churches will do well to adapt their own church culture now to address that which motivation theory calls self-actualization—becoming uniquely you, growing into what you were meant to be. This emphasis fits well under Jesus' teaching that he has come so that his followers may have life—life in all its fullness (John 10:10 TEV). Paul looked at his leadership task as preparing God's people for works of service that build up the body of Christ until they become all they can be, "reaching to the very height of Christ's full stature" (Ephesians 4:11–13 TEV). He saw himself as a gardener, planting seeds in individual lives that he expected would grow through the Spirit's work into self-actualizing, fruitful living.

Appealing to the more basic human needs did indeed enable the Spirit to energize Christian churches over the centuries. But human motivation alone has its limits, especially as our American culture becomes increasingly unchurched, because so many no longer see churches meeting needs they recognize. It is time to learn how to appeal to the supernatural motivation offered by the Holy Spirit.

Needing to focus on the practical, personal payoff of participating in a local church partnership provides good reason to rediscover two aspects of Paul's ministry that were left on the periphery once Christian churches became well established, centuries ago. One is his emphasis on the gifts and fruit of the Spirit. The other is his leadership self-image as a gardener and a builder, rather than a shepherd. Spiritual gifts will be explored more in chapter 3. More on ministry as gardening is in chapter 4.

REASON PLUS FEELINGS

The opposite of having feelings for something or someone is apathy; literally, being without passion. So many traditional churches today are victims of apathy. Members don't care the way they used to, which means that younger generations carry fewer positive associations with church life. To be apathetic about something is soon to see it as irrelevant to what is personally important. Evidence of their growing irrelevance is on display among withering traditional congregations.

In general, traditions emerge when they offer participants positive, rewarding experiences, and traditions die out when current participants no longer find those experiences satisfying. The challenge is to find new ways to offer positive religious experiences in churches.

Diane Butler Bass is a popular speaker whose interpretation of larger movements helps explain to mainline churches their continuing decline. She observes that to put the words "experiential" and "belief" in the same sentence is asking for trouble in those circles. Noting how the modern Pentecostal movement first gave expression to the priority of experience, she reports the reaction of one pastor: "You mean we're all going to become Pentecostals? My congregation would rather die first! Faith isn't about feelings. It has to have intellectual content." Or as another said, "Why is it that the choice among churches always seems to be the choice between intelligence on ice and ignorance on fire?"[6] This dilemma, of course, is false. Between these extremes many congregations are working out a healthy middle ground.

What could be so wrong anyway with emotional experiences in church? Here is the issue: do the emotions come first, before you rationally figure them out? Such "raw" emotions are too often not of the Spirit and can become destructive. Or do feelings flow from perceptions subject to reason, based on Scriptures? Such feelings can be the bedrock of church life. Psychologists call the first somatic, body-based theory and the second cognitive, brain-based theory.

New Testament scholar Matthew Elliott observes that theologians over the centuries worked from a somatic theory and therefore rejected emotions as irrational and unimportant. They picked up this understanding from Greek philosophy, like Stoicism, that focused on living at a level of reason higher than just emotions.

But the whole endeavor of psychological counseling today works with cognitive theory, based on the assumption that emotions can be changed by changing perceptions of their cause and that such change is subject to reasoning. Elliott would label Paul's fruit of the Spirit—such as love, joy, peace—as faithful feelings, the title of his book. In his study of emotions in the New Testament, he highlights how heartfelt convictions of the mind are accompanied by movement into action. Faithful feelings are an important part of the blessings God gives by way of the Holy Spirit.[7]

The role of emotions is important today because so many Spirit-oriented Christians, called Pentecostals, concentrate on them. For Word-oriented churches, these feelings need to be in the proper sequence: facts followed by faith followed by feelings. The *facts* are proclaimed in the Word. *Faith* is not only the noun for beliefs but is especially the verb for trusting those facts about God. God-pleasing *feelings* then flow from such faith. Spiritual leaders can be more confident in their ministry when they expect the Holy Spirit to work through this progression. Spirit-oriented churches would agree on the flow but are inclined especially to emphasize the third-stage feelings that can become very emotional. They often arrange their time together in ways that seemingly place primary emphasis on emotions.

Modern English does not lend itself well to naming what can be loosely described today as feelings, emotions, or human spirit. That territory was defined several centuries ago as "affections" by American theologian Jonathan Edwards. For him, affections are strong inclinations of the soul that are manifested in thinking, feeling, and acting. Affections are different from emotions, which can be fleeting, superficial, and irrationally overpowering.[8] For our times think of "feelings" in the broad sense of being subject to reason and of motivating into action This will be important when we get to fruit of the Spirit in chapter 3.

PSYCHOLOGY OF RELIGIOUS EXPERIENCE

A whole psychology of religious experience has emerged in academia to research and understand experiences loosely categorized as religious.

A hundred years ago, James Williams, the first academic to take the title "psychologist," gave classic descriptions of religious experiences. He used such phrases as "an incomparable feeling of happiness which is connected with the near presence of God's spirit" and "a sense of a presence, strong, and at the same time soothing, which hovers over me."[9]

Of special interest will be studies of peak experiences like "conversion." Ralph W. Wood shows that experience of any sort must be described to be recognized. Language facilitates awareness and helps make it conscious.[10] Hence the need to "name it" when an experience happens.

What kind of a special vocabulary can be used to recognize and talk about the Spirit at work around us? One phrase is "Spirit encounter." If you want to say spiritual experience, remember to capitalize the S, so all know you are talking about an experience of the Holy Spirit. Other good phrases are "a God moment" or "a Holy Spirit sighting." An "awakening" is a helpful word for those very special and rare times when one's Christian faith takes on significantly more meaning—when God becomes more real and personal in a new way, an "aha" experience when a light bulb goes on and life in Christ takes on a whole new dimension. It is comparable to the Evangelical word "conversion," only awakenings can happen more than once in a lifetime. Awakenings will be developed in chapter 6.

Addressing the classical conversion of someone who was not a Christian, H. Newton Malony concludes that first, human beings are so constructed that decisions made individually will not last, and second, the confirmation and support of others may be necessary for a conversion to be effective.[11] Hence the need to "share it"—to describe to others our personal encounters with the Holy Spirit when they happen. In Luther's terms, mutual conversation and consolation of the brethren is one of the basic means of grace by which God, through his Word, offers counsel and help.[12]

More recent psychological research on conversion recognizes there is a gradual conversion in addition to the classic sudden and even dramatic conversion. J. T. Richardson suggests that this second type is more rational than emotional; it flows from a compassionate rather than stern theology; and it emerges from a search for meaning and purpose.[13] Life-changing conversion to Christian faith does happen to some people at a specific time and place. But for most, it is a process of growth in grace, with perhaps several memorable awakenings along the way.

Again, you will see more of the Spirit's movement if you have words to describe what happened, and you share this with others. J. Harold Ellens, the pastor and psychologist quoted earlier, describes those moments as "unique encounters when you can just feel something extraordinary happened that can only be attributed to the Spirit. Call them experiences of the Spirit, or special Spirit encounters." He goes on to explain that

> The Holy Spirit is always a mystery, an intriguing agent of God, full of intimations of God's nature, truth, and grace. These intimations speak spontaneously to our natures as we hunger for God. In this process, the spirit is always evident, sometimes only in retrospect, always better than we thought it could be. One must have the eyes to see and the ears to hear, of course.

That is, these things are evident to those living life close the wind, expecting the progress that comes from a vital spiritual quest. It is an intriguing and exciting thing indeed to live life always consciously anticipating how the Holy Spirit of God will show up around the next corner. The Spirit always does if we are expecting it.[14]

A major role of church culture is to offer language for identifying and explaining personal religious experiences. Christian hymns and songs have always served that function, as do the Psalms. As church cultures undergo change, Christian church leaders need to take responsibility to highlight special descriptive language that can help believers express personal feeling aroused by the Spirit. More will be said about this in chapter 6. They also need to teach discernment of what is from the Spirit and what may not be. Reliable signs of the Spirit's influence are discussed in chapter 2.

Encounters with the Spirit are more common than many think. I bring my own research through a survey of prayer life of over five hundred randomly selected ordinary Lutherans. About half said they regularly experience a deep sense of *peace* and the strong *presence* of God during prayer. Striking was that about half agreed that "Prayer is the most satisfying experience of my life."[15] These numbers were much higher than I and most of my pastor colleagues anticipated and gave direction to my thinking over the last twenty years.

Traditional churches typically do little to encourage ordinary Christians to gain confidence and hope through sharing these personal experiences. We can change this.

GIVE SPIRITUAL FELLOWSHIP PRIORITY OVER CHURCH ORGANIZATION

The congregations Paul led were truly spiritual fellowships—partnerships of believers drawn together by special motivation of the Holy Spirit and in which the Holy Spirit dwells (Ephesians 2: 22). They made up whatever minimal level of formal organization they needed to solve problems they encountered, like how to make sure the Greek-speaking widows in their fellowship received as much support as the local Hebrew-speaking widows. For this, they formally appointed seven Greek-speaking helpers, including Stephen (Acts 6).

Informal fellowships stand in contrast to the formal organizational structures that specialize in writing out various roles and relationships, as in a constitution. Extensive formal organization of churches rose to prominence, especially in the recent half century, with the explosive growth of management as a discipline for corporations and other enterprises.

It is no surprise, then, that churches, beginning in the 1950s and '60s, faced a major temptation to become a formalized organization, like so many social clubs with their members, volunteers, and committees. But the danger is that organizational methods will squeeze out awareness of Spirit-led ways of Christian fellowship. Because of the rise of the management mentality, organizational ways and the ways of the Spirit are in tension as never before in church history. The church leadership challenge in the twenty-first century is to find a middle ground that keeps the freshness of the Spirit-fed fellowship and the consistency of organizational structures that do not erect barriers to the Spirit.

Many churches were primed to apply new management techniques to their church leadership in the 1960s to 1980s. In 1986, I coauthored a book on *Pastoral Administration: Integrating Ministry and Management*[16] that sold well. But judging by the results through the 1990s and first decade of 2000, that emphasis was not productive. Historic mainline churches were most interested. But their continued and accelerating decline forces the issue of what is wrong. In retrospect, they hitched their future to a then-new leadership model with limited application to churches, because it does not recognize the empowering resource of the Holy Spirit.

Spirit-oriented leadership of church organizational structures will be even more important in the future because of the new trend for just a few churches to become very large. Most of the growth in Protestantism is happening in those mega-churches, as documented by the Hartford Institute for Religion Research.[17] Churches do not get big because they are well organized by human standards that reflect other current trends in society. They get big because the Spirit propels them, and their organizational structure facilitates—rather than hinders—this foundational growth.

Where the Rest of This Book Goes

The next chapter presents further descriptions of religious experiences as Part I's focus on the benefits of recognizing encounters with the Spirit today. Part II has two chapters that present the biblical framework for what to expect of the Spirit and how he works. Part III shifts to the crucial subject of how to seek more encounters with the Spirit, both personally and as a congregation. Part IV addresses congregations that are moved to modify their present church culture to become more oriented to the work of the Holy Spirit in their midst.

Here is a summary of the positive behaviors to aim for in changing a church's culture. Congregations are encouraged to ask the Father to send the Spirit in specific ways. Tell stories of how the Spirit worked recently. Celebrate progress in personal spiritual journeys, especially in the form of major awakenings to a higher level of spiritual understanding. Offer a greater variety of opportunities for encounters with the Spirit. Be willing to recognize God's supernatural interventions in healings. Make a conscious decision to cultivate soil for the Holy Spirit and to remove church-culture barriers that block him. Then the Holy Spirit can do more of his refreshing, renewing work among those gathered as the congregation.

Churches in decline need to address this basic issue. Is theirs somehow a God problem? Has he lost relevance in our increasingly secular society? Or is the problem really with a church's inherited culture for approaching God and receiving what he offers? Chapter 3 presents good evidence that God is alive and well and that Christianity is currently growing rapidly around the world in forms that emphasize the Holy Spirit. Let this fact be a call for traditional Word-oriented Protestants to seek new ways to open themselves to the Spirit's renewing influence today.

CHAPTER 2

How Do People Experience God in Their Lives?

The Holy Spirit shapes human spirit.

—JOHN 3: 6

The Advocate, the Holy Spirit, whom the Father
will send in my name, will teach you all things and
will remind you of everything I have said to you.

—JOHN 14: 26

Is there a more basic question for Christians and their leaders to ask in this twenty-first century than, how do people experience God in their lives today? Ways of previous generations are not working as well in younger generations. Word-oriented churches rightfully insist that the facts about God's ways are objectively true. The question is how they become subjectively true for individuals. When and how do believers attach trust and feelings to the gospel? Faith without feelings remains superficial and probably boring.

Biblically, it is the Holy Spirit's work to bring hearers of the Word to such subjective experiences. This is the job description Jesus offered to Nicodemus, who approached him one night to seek better understanding of what this new rabbi was teaching.

Jesus explained he was all about the coming of the kingdom of God that you cannot see, without being born again. Nicodemus was really curious and asked, "How can a man be born when he is old? He cannot enter a second time into his mother's womb to be born." Jesus answered, "You must be born again of water and the Spirit, but the Spirit gives birth to spirit" (John 3:6 NIV). Another version of that last phrase is "A person is born physically of human parents but is born spiritually of the Spirit" (TEV). Over time the Spirit shapes human spirit.

Touching human spirits is the Holy Spirit's job. Spirit is a well-used word, the meaning of which is hard to pin down. But we know a highly "spirited" person when we see one. The opposite is to be discouraged, which describes a condition of the heart. Other words for a low spirit are depressed, anxious, unloved, or gloomy. Significant here is that their opposite is what Paul describes as the fruit of the Spirit, the major subcategory of gifts of the Spirit. These fruit include love, joy, trust, peace, and patience. While these can be described as human qualities or characteristics, they are best regarded as feelings that express a heart condition. They are deeper than head knowledge. According to the apostle Paul, God puts his Spirit in our hearts, (2 Corinthians 1:22).

"Spirit," in the original, means wind. Jesus pointed out that you cannot see the wind, but you can hear it (John 3:8). We might add that we can see the wind's effects in the movement of leaves and in the coolness a gentle breeze brings. How the natural wind blows is something we can identify with our senses of sight, hearing, and touch. The wind makes differences that are "sensible," or observable. Observable, too, are changes the Spirit wind can bring to the feelings of believers. This heart work is in addition to head work, by which the Spirit enlightens believers with better knowledge of what the Word teaches.

Imagine yourself as Nicodemus. The practical question I am asking on your behalf is, how does the Holy Spirit work today in my life and my congregation? What observable differences should I look for? How can I prepare myself so the Spirit can do his special work better?

THE HEART LANGUAGE OF GOD'S PEOPLE

The Bible presents many facts about God and how he relates to the humans he created. It teaches such basics as sinful human nature and the salvation won for us by Jesus on the cross, now offered by God's grace. We learn about the next world, where the life of God's people will be even more abundant that it is now. We can learn from the Bible about the many promises God makes to his people. The details are worked out in doctrine books. These address head knowledge.

To find out how God's people feel about his actions and promises, we need to turn to language different from logical propositional truths. Feelings are expressed best in images and metaphors of poetry. The book of Psalms is the best source for this kind of inspired heart language. Psalm 23, "The Lord is my shepherd," is the best and most beloved psalm for putting words to feelings—the feelings engendered by the Holy Spirit. Here is an interpretation that stresses feelings:

With God as my shepherd I *feel full* of all I need. In him I find the *peace* of lying in a green pasture and walking along a quiet stream. My anxious soul is *refreshed* by him. He gives me the *confidence* to walk in paths of right behavior. He *takes away fear* when I face uncertainty and *comforts* me with his presence. I feel his *powerful love* when he provides for me in hard times and assures me I am special. He provides such abundance that *my cup overflows with blessings*. I *trust* he will always love and bless me with goodness. How great it is to feel the *presence* of the Lord, now and forever.

Three key words can summarize what the Spirit brings to God's people: peace, presence, and power. Do Christians always feel at peace with God and the world? Of course not. Our sinful nature often causes us to feel anxious and unloved. Are Christians always confident that God is present, comforting us throughout our daily lives? Of course not. Our human nature is to trust only ourselves. Do Christians always feel the power of God working things out on their behalf? Of course not. Satan wants us to depend only on our own meager powers.

But there are times when these positive feelings of peace, presence, and power rise up in our consciousness. Such times can seem like breakthroughs when a new, refreshing mood shoves aside an old, sour mood. This is the Holy Spirit touching human spirit. You can notice the difference in yourself and in others. We can learn to recognize shifts toward more love, joy, peace, trust, patience, kindness, gentleness, faithfulness, goodness, and self-control. This is the fruit the Spirit works to grow in God's people.

RECOGNIZING THE SPIRIT'S WORK YOUR LIFE

The apostle Paul had a dramatic experience of God and also a slow, over-the-years formation by the Holy Spirit. The dramatic one is his well-known conversion on his journey to Damascus in Acts 9. We note that God sent Ananias to help him understand and share what happened. The slower formation, we know little about. It started with the three years he spent in the desert after his conversion, a place Jesus, too, sought out before he started his ministry. According to Paul's report in Galatians, a total of fourteen years (Galatians 2:1) passed before he went to Jerusalem with Barnabas, who had sought him out in his hometown of Tarsus and supervised a year of ministry internship (Acts 11:25). It is reasonable to expect that Paul spent a lot of his unrecorded years explaining to others what happened to him and even preaching in the Galatian region near his home in Tarsus. Somewhere in those years, Paul had worked out the centrality of grace in God's relationship with his people, as evidenced so powerfully at his conversion. He also came to much greater depth of understanding of how the Spirit works changes in the believer's heart, as the Spirit did in his own. Paul is by far the clearest and most applied interpreter of God's grace in action.

When he writes about what the Holy Spirit can do among God's people, you can confidently assume this is what the Spirit did to him over those years. He learned to look into the future based on his own past experiences of the Spirit. You, too, can do that.

✓ Have you found that your understanding of faith has moved beyond childhood knowledge to greater willingness to live with Jesus as Lord of all your life? That was the Holy Spirit at work (1 Corinthians 12:3).

✓ Have you found that certain desires of your sinful flesh have lessened and even gone away? You experienced how, living with the Holy Spirit, you were less inclined to gratify desires of your old sinful nature (Galatians 5:16).

✓ Have you experienced feelings of enslavement to pervasive fears that inhibit joyful living? The Spirit lessens them as he helps you cry "Daddy," confident of yourself as his child (Romans 8:15). Is there movement in that direction that you have noticed in yourself lately?

✓ Have you noticed yourself more inclined to be involved in a congregation, perhaps teaching Sunday school or taking on administrative responsibilities? The Holy Spirit has been working on you, giving you extra motivation to do what you now find to be satisfying (1 Corinthians 12:7).

✓ Have you found yourself experiencing a spiritual act of worship in decisions to sacrifice what seemed important, in order to live a life more pleasing to God? (Romans 12:1). Recognize the Spirit at work.

✓ Have you experienced a special sense of unity with other Christians, perhaps in a time of worship or when decisions were made? That was the Holy Spirit at work. Have you experienced such unity at a special conference with Christians? Thank the Spirit (Ephesians 4:3–6).

✓ Have you found, this week or last month, a greater sense of love, joy, peace, patience, or gentleness? That was the Spirit working these fruit in your life. In years of teaching the fruit of the Spirit, I found that the fruit that people want more than any other is patience, especially those with children. Have you become more patient with your children lately? That's the Spirit. Do you want more patience? Ask the Father to send his Spirit.

✓ Have you found yourself frustrated, speaking only words of human wisdom and seeking opportunities to express spiritual truths in spiritual words? (1 Corinthians 2:13). This tug helped me recognize that as well as I was doing, I was not at home at a secular university and should teach at a Lutheran university. It also explains the satisfaction and joy I find in turning insights from psychology of religion into spiritual words.

Can you prove that any of these positive movements in your life came from the Holy Spirit? No more so than you can prove God exists to someone who does not want to see him. This insight happens when the eyes of your heart are enlightened (Ephesians 1:18). It takes the Spirit to recognize what the Spirit has done in your life. This is what Jesus taught Nicodemus: You cannot enter the kingdom of God unless you are born of water and the Spirit. The Holy Spirit does give new birth to human spirit (John 3:6).

RECOGNIZING THE SPIRIT'S WORK IN OTHERS

✓ Wherever someone encounters Christ's call to follow and hears the good news of grace in Christ, there is the Holy Spirit at work. Where a believer participates in that encounter through personal witness and life, there is the Spirit in abundance.

✓ Wherever presentations of the Word bring greater insights and illumination to someone, there is the Holy Spirit at work, especially so when greater understanding is awakened in the heart (Ephesians 1:18).

✓ Wherever a believer's new life in Christ becomes stronger and more evident, there is the Holy Spirit at work. Look for him working this outcome, especially through means of "the mutual conversation and consolation of brethren," in Luther's phrase.[18]

✓ Wherever a person is considering whether or not to attend church on a Sunday morning and feels the tug to do so, there is the Holy Spirit at work, especially so when relationships with others in the fellowship help bring that affirmative response.

✓ Wherever two or three come together in the name of Christ, there he is in a special way, through the Holy Spirit (Matthew 18:20). Look for the Spirit's work in improved relationships within a congregation and beyond it.

✓ Wherever there is special boldness, or wisdom, or determination among Christians, there is the Holy Spirit in special ways. Luke, writer of the third Gospel and Acts, describes followers with such characteristics as being "filled with the Holy Spirit."[19] This description can be applied today to church members recognized as having special wisdom, courage, or faith.

✓ The Spirit also brings freedom, and his work can be seen whenever a follower of Christ finds new levels of joy and peace through release from guilt and expectations of perfection (2 Corinthian 3:17).

✓ Wherever Christians come together with special energy and sing with gusto and intensity, there is the Holy Spirit (Colossians 3:16).

"Spirit team" is a new name for cheerleaders at sporting events. When God's Spirit touches human spirits, the joy can be like that of a high-energy event happening among those gathered in the name of Christ.

✓ Consider this viewpoint of Paul's for spotting the Holy Spirit: The hallmark of the Spirit is freshness and renewal. God promises the Spirit will put a *new* heart and a *new* spirit into his people (Ezekiel 36:26). Paul tells the Romans that the Spirit brings *new* ways different from living by rules (Romans 8:1–4). He tells the Corinthians that *new* life-giving relationships come through the *new* covenant of the Spirit (2 Corinthians 3:6).

Some would understand the new life brought by the Spirit as a one-time event—at conversion. But Luther understood it as a frequent, even daily process of drowning out the old nature in us through repentance and letting the new nature come forth and arise. Being made new again—renewal—is the Holy Spirit's work (Titus 3:5). The Spirit's way is movement, not status quo.

Paul explains to the Corinthians that the Holy Spirit transforms us into Christlikeness with the movement of "ever increasing glory" (2 Corinthians 3:18). We are to be thus transformed by the renewing of our minds (Romans 12:2). The Spirit does that with individuals. But he also can do so with congregations. The work of getting members aligned with Christ and with each other for ministries that build up the body of Christ should have the goal of reaching together to the very heights of the fullness of Christ (Ephesians 4:13). Whatever an individual Christian or a congregation might be reaching for now, there is more the Spirit wants to give and do. Settling for existing conditions is not the preferred outcome for life in the Spirit.

LESS OBVIOUS RELIGIOUS EXPERIENCES

One of the greatest Roman Catholic theologians of our times, Karl Rahner, wrote *The Spirit in the Church* in 1977. It was his effort to put perspective on the charismatic movement that was strong, especially among Catholics, Lutherans, and Episcopalians in the 1960s and '70s. Those in the movement often had overwhelming experiences of the Holy Spirit in their personal lives, reflected in very joyful singing and dancing, intense prayer and usually speaking in tongues. Rahner responded, yes, but remember the Spirit usually works in normal ways. In fact, often his presence is not obvious.

According to Rahner, the Spirit of grace and freedom can work in a Christian even in the following unglamorous ways:

✓ When a person does his or her duty where it can only be done, with the terrible feeling that he or she is doing something ludicrous that no one will thank him for.

✓ When a person is really good to another person, from whom no echo of understanding and thankfulness can be heard.

✓ Where a person obeys not because he or she must and would otherwise find it inconvenient to disobey, but purely on account of that inconceivable thing called the will of God.

✓ Where the leap into the darkness of death is accepted as the beginning of everlasting promise.

✓ Where one dares to pray into a silent darkness and knows that one is heard, although no answer seems to come back.[20]

In 2007, the media spread the news of an apparent crisis of faith in Mother Teresa. This information came from a book containing a letter she wrote to her spiritual confidant:

Jesus has a very special love for you. [But] as for me, the silence and the emptiness is so great, that I look and do not see,—listen and do not hear— the tongue moves [in prayer] but does not speak ... I want you to pray for me—that I let Him have [a] free hand.

Her spiritual superiors, however, considered this a spiritual strength—that she could persist in her calling, even without feelings of affirmation from God. Such commitment could only come from the Spirit's movement in her life.[21]

We Protestants have a lot to learn from Christians of a church culture very different from ours, where duty, obedience, and even grim determination can be spiritual acts. This may open up new appreciation for our church ancestors of previous generations who did not focus on emotions of joy and for whom love of others was sometimes hard to see.

WHISPERS OF THE HOLY SPIRIT

We can envision God as a father and Jesus as a son. How do you envision a spirit? At Jesus' baptism, Mark tells us that the Spirit came down on him like a dove. I have come to think of the Holy Spirit as a dove, sitting on my shoulder and whispering into my ear. Christian living is a process of learning, over time, to listen to the Spirit's whispers.

Readying the disciples for his crucifixion and ascension, Jesus told them the Father would replace him with another advocate, the Spirit of Truth. "You know him because he lives with you and will be in you" (John 14: 16,17). "The Holy

Spirit will teach you all things and will remind you of everything I have said to you" (John 14: 26). The original word, *parakletos*, can be translated as comforter or counselor. A better choice is *advocate*. The Spirit is God's advocate in our lives. The Spirit communicates in whispers we can easily fail to hear.

The Power of a Whisper is a recent publication of Bill Hybels, senior pastor of Willow Creek Community Church. He is very cautious and even defensive about "God told me" language. He tells how he personally hears God as a whisper and writes about many of his whisper experiences, as well writing whisper stories of others he knows.

Hybels writes, "From Genesis to Revelation, the constant refrain of Scriptures declares that our faith is relational—God listens when we speak through prayer, and we are to listen when he speaks through his whispers. In that earlier era, I longed for a sense of whispers like those, and thankfully, over time, I would learn to hear them."[22]

For me, the clearest "God told me" experience came when I was considering a possible call to plant a church in my hometown of Cleveland, Ohio. A lot of pieces of the puzzle of where next to go came together at about four o'clock on a Monday afternoon. That evening, I announced to the family at supper that God told me where we were going next. Until then, I had personally never used that phrase. Later, with all the frustrations and disappointments of church planting, I drew comfort and energy from being convinced this is what God wanted me to do.

I recently experienced a loud whisper from the Holy Spirit in work I have been doing with our sister church body in Haiti. On a trip to a church site in a city damaged by the 2010 earthquake, we were envisioning how much better the work of ministering to others and of building houses would go if we had a guesthouse for visiting teams. I can remember exactly where I was standing when I had this strong urge to put down a significant amount of money to buy property for this guesthouse. The whisper said to talk to a specific woman in our group. So I asked her if she could put down the same amount. It was a short exchange: if you do, I will. We did. With the help of World Relief and Human Care, a division of the Lutheran Church—Missouri Synod, there are now two guesthouses in different cities that were damaged by the earthquake. That initial investment proved crucial to starting the momentum that brought these results, plus three houses.

Go back to the image of the Holy Spirit, like a dove, sitting on your shoulder, whispering and advocating what God wants in your life. To be a biblical Christian, you also need to imagine someone else sitting on your other shoulder. Satan is God's adversary who wants to separate us from him. Peter gives us the image of a roaring lion, seeking whom he may devour (1 Peter 5:8). Pick your favorite image of the adversary but preferably something more realistic than a red devil with a pitchfork and tail. The Internet world is used to designing symbolic avatars. I like to envision Satan as an ugly, crabby guy who is always whining.

When you do hear a whisper that gets your attention, how can you determine if it is the Holy Spirit or the crabby, whining foe?

In his discussion of *Hearing God,* Dallas Willard presents the three-lights test, originally named for finding a safe entrance into a difficult harbor in Italy. When all three are aligned in the same direction, you can grow in confidence that an intended action is God's will. The lights are:

- ✓ the circumstances you find yourself in, by God's providence;
- ✓ the impressions of the Spirit—what we are calling the whispers of the Spirit; and
- ✓ Scriptural standards.

In the words of Frederick Meyer, "God's impressions *within* and his word *without* are always corroborated by his providence *around.*" These are the three lights that, combined, give guidance for discerning God's voice. Willard discusses extensively how these are not a formula that can be simplistically applied, for each of those lights takes spiritual experience to recognize.[23]

I would add a fourth source of guidance in determining who is whispering into your ear—the counsel of well-experienced Christians. Certainly for major decisions, when you think the three lights are in alignment, wisdom lies in the request that other experienced Christians reflect on your assessments.

Where the Holy Spirit comes, there is enthusiasm. But it might be just the human energy and excitement that good cheerleaders can evoke. How do you know it is truly in-Spirited? Denial can easily carry the day among those who are not used to looking for the Spirit. The apostle Paul would counsel that you really have to look for evidence of the Spirit through eyes of faith. But such eyes only come through the work of the Holy Spirit. Isn't this just a circular argument? In human terms, yes. But Paul would say, so be it. You are really addressing actions of God that are beyond simple human understanding and yet apparent to those enlightened by the Holy Spirit.

After years of discussion, the time came for the board of our church to make the decision about whether and how much to build and how much to borrow, in what was the third major building project in ten years. There were good arguments for and against the proposal. Opinions were strong on both sides. The meeting had the potential to result in major conflict. But not so. Full consensus emerged with enthusiasm to go ahead. I could not help but recognize that the Holy Spirit, the dove of peace, was present. It helped that at the same time, in a different room, the director of prayer ministries had gathered a group that was praying for clear direction.

RELIABLE SIGNS OF THE HOLY SPIRIT

In his first letter, John warns his friends, "Do not believe every spirit, but test the spirits to see whether they are from God." What is the test? "This is how you can recognize the Spirit of God: Every spirit that acknowledges that Jesus Christ has come in the flesh is from God, but every spirit that does not acknowledge Jesus is not from God" (1 John 4: 1-3).

In addition to the three-light test, more practical guidance comes from Jonathan Edwards, powerful preacher and prominent Reformed theologian, in what is now recognized as the first Great Awakening in eighteenth-century New England.

A second and a third Great Awakening occurred in nineteenth-century America. The Pentecostal movement of the twentieth century is considered by some to be a fourth Great Awakening. The core controversial issue in all four revivals remained the same. One side emphasized religious emotions as the essence; one's feeling the love of God was most important. The other taught that the heart of true religion is right thinking; emotions are fickle and often lead astray.

Jonathan Edwards was decidedly Word oriented. He argued against a shallow, human-oriented view of spirituality. As noted in the introductory chapter, Edwards insisted that religious experience is centered in what he called the "affections"—strong inclinations of the soul that are manifested in thinking, feeling, and acting. "Soul" meant the deepest and most essential part of the human person—what the Bible calls the "heart."

Affections can be either good or bad. The difference is that the good lead us toward God and the bad away from God. It is important to not be misled by bad or shallow affections, which Jonathan Edwards went at length to describe. While such affections can be a genuine manifestation of the Spirit, each can have other explanations, such as prideful, show-off quoting of many Scripture passages, or self-serving eloquent talk and passionate praise for God, or pharisaical devotion to religious activities. This is not to say such activities are false. But they can have other motivations and in themselves are less than reliable indicators of the Spirit. They need to be accompanied by more reliable signs that reflect a closer relationship with Christ. Some examples of reliable signs are:

✓ a lasting indwelling of the Holy Spirit that produces a new nature, apparent through lives that show a difference;

✓ a new spiritual sense reflected in love of God that does not come from self-interest;

✓ a new kind of convicted knowing and genuine humility;

✓ a hunger for God and a Christlike Spirit; and

✓ Christian practice.[24]

HOW DO YOU GET MORE OF THE SPIRIT?

"Growing in grace and knowledge" is an intriguing phrase Paul's colleague, the apostle Peter, used in giving a farewell wish to those reading his second letter. We recognize how to bring about growth in knowledge. On our own, we can gain more knowledge of Scripture geography and history, and was can master dictionary definitions of biblical words.

But how do we grow in grace? Grace is not under our control the way we can gain knowledge on our own, with time and determination. By definition, grace is a gift given freely. This is the meaning of the word we use to translate the Greek *charis*—gift by grace. God, through the Spirit, initiates gifts that allow us to grow in our capacity to become more Christlike. This happens as we discover greater readiness to energetically serve others (gifts of the Spirit) and as we experience changes in our feelings of love and joy in all their forms (fruit of the Spirit).

The root for the word *charis* is *chara*, which means joy or gladness. *Chara* is the word used in Greece today to wish a blessing on someone else; it is a wish for someone's well-being. God's grace is meant for your well-being. If you want more of the blessing of joy and the other good fruit, put yourself where the Holy Spirit can work on you and give you the lasting fruit that comes only from above.

You can't get to the grace for Christian living and service on your own. It is not something someone can command you to do. Inspirational messages can bring a day or two of change, but lasting growth in love, peace, patience, and other godly fruit, as well as in the joy of serving others, has to come as a gift of God through his Holy Spirit.

So how do you get more of these gifts? In short, you ask for the Spirit to work on you and change your heart, and then you put yourself where the Spirit can get to you and do his heart-changing work, step by step. You do that by staying tuned to God's Word and staying in the company of other Christians. This is how you grow in grace.

You will get even more of the Holy Spirit when you are ready to recognize he is indeed supernaturally present today. Was the special measure of the Spirit's work true only for Bible people in Bible times? I grew up learning that the miracles in the Bible were only true for that time, but once the Christian church was established, miracles no longer happened. Hence, don't expect any today. The same filters led me to see that being full of the Holy Spirit is something that happened only in Bible times. Hence, you cannot expect special interventions of God today. Hence, everything in church life today is under human control, with some symbolic reference to God the Holy Spirit.

Are you willing to join Paul in the belief that God's way of interacting with people is true for all times in the Christian church? His way is by sending his Spirit to influence personal lives and the church partnerships these believers form. Thriving church life is not under our direct control. When we try to do church on our own, our routines tend to turn into something so humanly ordinary that few would recognize anything special of the Holy Spirit in it. Thriving in the Spirit comes at God's initiative. Our job is to prepare the soil of church life so the Holy Spirit can best do his advocacy and influence. More on this in chapter 5.

PART II
The Biblical Framework for Recognizing the Spirit at Work

CHAPTER 3
Seek the Gifts and Fruit of the Spirit

> Now about spiritual gifts, brothers, I
> do not want you to be ignorant.
> —1 CORINTHIANS 12:1

> The fruit of the Spirit is love, joy, peace,
> patience, kindness, goodness, faithfulness,
> gentleness and self-control.
> —GALATIANS 5:22

Of all the cities where he ministered, the apostle Paul stayed the longest in Ephesus. For the two and a half years there, he was, in effect, running a practical seminary for church planters "in the lecture hall of Tyrannus" (Acts 19:9). Many of his "disciples" would lead congregations or would go on to plant new ones. Some certainly would have been linked to the other six congregations described in the book of Revelation, all of which were within a hundred miles of Ephesus.

Imagine daily discussions about solving church problems, like those they kept hearing about in the new church in Corinth that Paul started several years earlier. The questions they would be asking would certainly include these: What makes a Christian church different from all the other religious clubs so prevalent in Roman cities? We understand God as Father and Son, but how does the Holy Spirit fit in? What can we expect from the Spirit? Where should we look to see this Spirit at work?

FOUR BASICS FROM PAUL ABOUT THE SPIRIT AT WORK IN A CONGREGATION

Paul's summary from these discussions appears in the twelfth chapter of his first letter to the Corinthians. He explains his purpose in the first verse: "Now about matters of the Spirit, brothers, I do not want you to be ignorant."

His first teaching is that "No one can say Jesus is Lord except by the Holy Spirit." Thus, the Holy Spirit has already been at work, moving any and all believers into saving faith. Such faith comes at God's initiative.

Second, he teaches to be aware of *charisma* given by the Holy Spirit. The gift given is *charis*. A gift *received* becomes *charisma*. The plural for gifts received is *charismata*. Paul begins his discussion of different charismata by using two other phrases to describe what they look like. They are different *ministries of service* and different *energies* for doing them (1 Corinthians 12:5–6).

Third, these expressions of the Spirit are for the common good of the congregation (1 Corinthians 12:7). They are not giftings to individual believers to be enjoyed privately, perhaps as a sign of special status. They are given to the fellowship through individual participants, acting in service to others.

Fourth, a different and additional key emphasis in Paul's teaching about gifts given by the Spirit comes at the end of chapter 12 in his transition to the beloved chapter 13 on love. He distinguishes a subset of spiritual gifts that he calls the greater gifts for the most excellent way of living together as a congregation. Chief is love, without which fulfilling life together is difficult. To the Galatians he describes these as fruit of the Spirit. These outgrowths of the Spirit's work are character traits and the feelings that accompany them. All of them have to do with building up healthy and productive relationships, basic to church life.

Lost in the translation of *charisma* as a gift is recognition that we have Paul's second great teaching on grace—the English word usually used for *charis*, the gift given. The first, he states most clearly in Ephesians: "For it is by grace you have been saved, through faith—not by works, so that no one can boast." We are saved at God's initiative. In 1 Corinthians 12, he explains that we receive motivations as gifts given by the Spirit, at God's initiative. They are expressions of his grace. We do not earn them. But we can ask for them, recognize when they are given, and better prepare ourselves for more such giftings.

THE HOLY SPIRIT BRINGS SPECIAL ENERGY FOR MINISTRY

Paul's major point in 1 Corinthians 12 is that in each congregation of believers, the Spirit is already at work, motivating all participants to contribute different acts of ministry for the common good. Such gifting might begin with natural talent, but it is not a gift to the congregation until it is put to use in that church. It is not the individual who determines his or her special gifting but rather the congregation that discerns who does what well. This is motivation very different from reluctantly serving on a committee. When unique Spirit-giftedness of individuals becomes the basis for their service in the fellowship, they have a much higher sense of focused energy and Spirit-given satisfaction.

The leadership challenge is not only to identify special giftings but especially, then, to encourage and guide each participant to put his or her own gifting to work in the congregation, as we can see Paul doing in the twelfth chapter to the Romans. "If it [this gifting by the Spirit] is to serve, let him serve; if it is teaching, let him teach; if it is encouraging, let him encourage; if it is contributing to the needs of others, let him give generously; if it is leadership, let him govern diligently; if it is showing mercy, let him do it cheerfully" (Romans 12: 6-8).

So many traditional congregations today report in frustration, "We can't get anybody to do anything in church." This especially becomes a symptom of organizing like a social club, with many committees that annually need to recruit volunteers to be fitted into predetermined organizational boxes, whether or not they have spiritual motivation.

Paul's way is to start with individual believers who are specially motivated by the Spirit and guide them into productive ministry in the fellowship. The formal organization exists to shape and guide the spiritual fellowship. This primary fellowship is the church of Christ. The formal organization and governance structure are not the real church. They are human inventions that exist to serve their underlying spiritual partnership.

What are these *charismata*—giftings the Spirit distributes among individuals for the good of all in a congregation? They include unusual wisdom, knowledge, and faith, along with special abilities to preach, teach, administer, and heal. All cannot do everything equally well. There is nothing controversial about this observation. Giftings of this sort would be regarded as quite normal today.

Do you, the reader, have a special gifting from the Spirit for your involvement in a congregation? You can recognize such a gifting when you enjoy doing something in your church, and you receive affirmation that you do this well. Do you look forward to helping or serving others? Do you like to personally encourage others in their faith? Perhaps you receive affirmation that when you lead a project, you do it well, and you find this satisfying. Do you enjoy being generous with your resources? Do you look forward to opportunities to teach children or adults? Do you find satisfaction in fixing things in the church building?

The listings Paul gives in 1 Corinthians 12 and Romans 12 are meant as examples. In your own words, write down what you find satisfaction in doing at church. _____. But recognize that the second part of identifying your spiritual gift is to get affirmation from others that they appreciate what you are doing. Some take pleasure in singing but perhaps do not do this well. Without affirmation, be cautious about considering your talent as a special gifting of God for the congregation. Some want to lead but discover few want to follow them.

The next chapter will discuss the overall leadership challenge of encouraging diverse expressions of spiritual giftings in church life. Unity can become hard to maintain. Paul learned to seek and rely on the fruit of the Spirit's working on individual hearts to make them more loving, patient, and kind to each other. The opposite and easier way to reach and maintain unity is to hold expectations to the low minimum that all can do. But such a congregation will inevitably come up short on spiritual passions.

But Paul also affirmed the ability to speak in an unusual language. This gifting is not important enough to appear in his other listing of *charismata* in Romans 12. Word-oriented churches have special difficulty with the Spirit's gift of speaking in tongues, for the basic reason that it overrides the highly valued rational process; it is fundamentally nonrational. Indeed, speaking in tongues is, for many Pentecostals, a heart language that becomes an issue only when some regard it as superior to rational head-language, as Paul warns against.

So why not concentrate on cultivating the other more normal workings of the Spirit? Surely for centuries, congregations have recognized and appreciated those fellow participants through whom the Spirit works for the common good.

The Holy Spirit Brings Empowerment for Relationships

Paul's fourth basic teaching is about what fruit to expect from the Holy Spirit. He presents a listing in Galatians 5: love, joy, peace, patience, kindness, goodness, faithfulness, gentleness, and self-control. He says "fruit" in the singular, the outgrowth of the Holy Spirit's work within individuals. As with examples of gifts, these fruit are not an exhaustive list. Other terms like these show up in his other letters. A key one is peace, which comes from a mind controlled by the Spirit (Romans 8:6).

That these fruit are relationship-oriented is clarified in his benediction to the Corinthians, where he chose "fellowship" as the key characteristic of the Holy Spirit: "May the grace of the Lord Jesus Christ, and the love of God, and the *fellowship* of the Holy Spirit be with you all" (2 Corinthians 13:14). The action most characteristic of the Holy Spirit's work is to bring us into greater fellowship with the Father and the Son and then to make changes in us to prepare us for constructive relationships with others around us.

In sum, if you want to see the Holy Spirit at work around you, look for human behaviors that reflect gifts and fruit of the Spirit.

GIFTS AND FRUIT OF THE SPIRIT AS THE CORE OF PAUL'S UNDERSTANDING

What makes this book different from so many others on the Holy Spirit is its fresh understanding of Paul's teaching on the gifts and fruit of the Spirit. Ever since the Christian church got institutionalized in the fourth century, these teachings on the gifts of the Spirit have been left on the periphery of what is important for church life together. In its organizational form, the church made a sharp distinction between clergy and laity. The ordained clergy themselves were regarded as God's gift (Ephesians 4:11). Little was expected of the rest, the laity, whose role it was to participate in the rites and to support the clergy.

A new perspective emerged in the 1970s and '80s, when Pentecostal Christians put their special interest in the gift of speaking in tongues into the context of the larger teaching of all the gifts of the Spirit in 1 Corinthians 12. Consultants developed spiritual gift inventories for improving church leadership by trying to identify those participants with one or the other of the range of gifts. The straightforward action, then, is to encourage each to put his or her gifting by the Spirit into practice in the life of the congregation. This practical expectation is already a major shift away from the old understanding because of the assumption that leadership roles are open to all.

I have been teaching, applying, and writing about the themes of 1 Corinthians 12 and Galatians 5 for twenty-five years. The more I work with them, the more I see them moving from the periphery of Paul's thoughts to the very core of his theology and leadership approach. These gifts of the Spirit are his second great teaching on grace. First is salvation by grace through faith; second is abundant Christian living by grace.

WORD-ORIENTED AND SPIRIT-ORIENTED CHRISTIANS

The sixteenth-century Reformation yielded three major branches of Protestantism: Lutheran, Reformed (Calvinists), and Anglican (Episcopalian), whose descendants dominated Protestant Christianity up to and through the first half of the twentieth century. My roots are Lutheran.

Those in this Reformation heritage remain strongly oriented to using reason to interpret Scriptures as the authority for Christian faith and life, often appearing to discourage any emotions. Meanwhile, in the last half of the twentieth century, the Pentecostal movement came to prominence in America and worldwide. These Christians are strongly oriented to directly experiencing the Holy Spirit. Over the last one hundred years, traditional Word-oriented Christians and leaders have often clashed with Pentecostal Spirit-oriented Christians over the roles of reason and emotions in church life. Rediscovery of Paul's full understanding of spiritual gifts opens the way to narrowing the gap.

Circumstances of the sixteenth-century Christian church led the Reformers to shy away from fully developing biblical teachings on the third person of the Trinity. They feared the Spirit's work would get mixed in with the superstitions that were rife at that time. They also resisted radical interpretations of the freedom brought by the Spirit that could turn into social revolution, like the disastrous Peasant's Revolt in Germany in 1525. Luther wrote wonderful hymns to the Spirit before that year. Afterwards, the Spirit receded in his thinking. Human social control was highly valued by John Calvin, as he modeled theocracy in Geneva.

In effect, the Reformers set the dimmer dial of the light switch on low for the third person of the Trinity. It is time to move the dial up to receive more of the light and energy that the Holy Spirit can bring today. This book explores how churches of the Reformation can do that, while remaining faithful to their classical heritage. Besides Reformed and Lutheran, these mainline church bodies today include Presbyterian, Methodist, and Episcopalian. Highly Word-oriented Baptists can work at dialing up their dimmer switch, too.

The mainline churches are now often called "old line." Once dominant in American society, they all have been on a forty-year decline in membership, now at an accelerating rate. Meanwhile, Pentecostals are growing explosively worldwide. This is reason enough for classical Protestant churches to take another look at how to cultivate the work of the Holy Spirit in their midst.

All Christian churches recognize the third person of the Trinity, the Holy Spirit. In our classic traditions, we pray for the Spirit's special work to enlighten believers and to bring heartfelt changes. But we do not identify what the changes look like, nor do we celebrate such growth when it does occur. Our priority is to turn the lights on bright for head knowledge. Yet historically, we keep the dimmer switch dialed low for heart change. The challenge for low-expectation churches is to dial up the dimmer switch to expose more of the work of the Spirit in changing hearts.

Returning to the Earliest Church Charismatics

By any standard, the growth of Pentecostal expressions of Christianity has been phenomenal. A hundred years after its start in 1906, the movement worldwide was estimated to include 558,000,000 adherents. Some observers project it will reach one billion by 2025. Even secularists admit there seems to be an "S" (Spirit) factor at work in the continuing dramatic growth of this movement worldwide.[25]

In his study *Global Pentecostalism*, sociologist Donald Miller of the University of Southern California distinguishes five expressions of Pentecostalism. Several he calls "classical" in denominational expression. Most relevant here are the last two. To one he gives the title "Independent Neo-Pentecostal," often founded by religious entrepreneurs "who embrace the reality of the Holy Spirit and package it in ways that make sense to culturally attuned teens and young adults, as well as upwardly mobile people who did not grow up in the Pentecostal tradition." Miller considers them to be the cutting edge of the movement.[26]

The fifth type Miller distinguishes is "Proto-Charismatic Christians." They may be open to special manifestations of the Spirit but do not feature them. "They are simply attempting to follow the example of Jesus and the model of the early Christian church, which they see as being filled with manifestations of the Spirit." I propose that traditional Protestants resolve to become earliest church charismatics.

LEARNING FROM SPIRIT-ORIENTED CHRISTIANS

In what follows, I will try to make the best case for how we Word-oriented believers can learn to thrive in the Spirit and then teach these ways to others. What I offer is solidly based on Scripture and, in my view, does not contradict anything in classical Reformation theology.

I offer the simple premise that more effective ministry by Word-oriented congregations will happen as we figure out how to recognize and purposefully cultivate the work of the Holy Spirit we confess to be already in a congregation's midst. My aim is to point ways toward becoming "early-church charismatic Christians," cultivating the normal work of the Holy Spirit.

For many established church bodies, like Episcopalian, Lutheran, and Catholic, the word charismatic brings back bad memories of the "charismatic" movement of the 1960s and '70s that turned out to be very divisive in many congregations. But that was more than forty years ago. It is time to take a fresh look at the other charismata Paul taught and relied on.

Churches in decline need to ask this question: Is theirs a God problem or a church-culture problem? That there is dramatic Spirit-driven growth going on worldwide suggests God the Spirit is alive and still powerful. Church decline points to the conclusion that an inherited church culture is falling out of sync with our rapidly changing American culture.

The world is changing too fast around us to continue to overlook the power source that the apostle Paul relied on for the growth of the early church. The Spirit continues to energize new churches in other parts of the world. It is time for more of us to seek that special energy from on high in traditional American churches.

CHAPTER 4
The Spirit Brings Growth beyond Conformity

And we who reflect the Lord's glory are being
transformed into his likeness with ever-increasing
glory, which comes from the Lord, who is the Spirit.
—2 CORINTHIANS 3:18

You are God's garden. I planted the seed,
Apollos watered it, but God made it grow.
—1 CORINTHIANS 3:6, 9

Do not conform any longer to the pattern of this world,
but be transformed by the renewing of your mind.
—ROMANS 12: 1

My brothers and I used to spend summers back on the Illinois farms of various uncles and aunts who lived in the same community. Those summers exposed us to a very different lifestyle from what can be seen living in the suburbs today. I remember riding with a cousin on his morning run to pick up milk cans from farms. It seemed every other farm family was a relative, to a second or third degree. Such social fabric gives a tremendous sense of identity and belonging.

But there are drawbacks. Big-city people today do not know very well the dynamics of village life. Conformity is basic. Everyone knows and watches everyone. To be very different from others brings penalties. As the saying goes, the nail that sticks its head up gets hammered down. Tied to their farms, they all know they have to live together for the rest of their lives. It is safer to base unity on everybody doing the same thing than to take on the challenge of maintaining unity while recognizing different spiritual temperaments and different stages of spiritual growth among participants. Village church culture emphasizes passing the faith on in well-known traditional ways that become the basis of preserving unity.

These stable and confining relationships have major implications for how church is practiced in a village. The need for predictability tends to keep in the background the Holy Spirit who wants to shake up relationships and bring individual growth that increases diversity in a congregation. Villagers become wary and critical toward neighbors who upset the routines, especially those who report strong emotional experiences of God.

The conformity of village life shaped the cultures of churches that still carry their European roots. For centuries after the Reformation, about 85 percent of the population lived in rural settings. Such a high percentage of rural population held through to the end of the nineteenth century, even in America.

Village roots are apparent in church heritages that still talk about a congregation as a parish. This is a geographic term, and everybody living in the village boundaries was treated as a congregation, whether or not they took on formal membership. Traditional parish talk has little to do with a primary spiritual fellowship. Loyalty to the village church and its denomination can be assumed, and motivation by guilt can be effective.

The old ways, however, do not fit well the new reality. Now, American population is down to, at most, about 15 percent rural, meaning that about 85 percent live in urbanized areas. This huge demographic shift alone should call into question the value of village-shaped traditions.

In contrast to such conformity, the apostle Paul recognized that the hallmark of the Holy Spirit at work is freshness and change. Unfortunately, significant change is usually not welcomed in most traditional churches. Paul told the Romans, "Just as Christ was raised from the dead through the glory of the Father, we too may live a *new* life (Romans 6:4). Paul also expected the Spirit to bring ongoing discoveries of newness and freedom into the life of Christ's followers. To the Corinthians, he pointed out, "The Lord is the Spirit, and where the Spirit of the Lord is, there is freedom" (2 Corinthians 3:17)—the freedom to break out of old ways and to try new ways of living and relating to God.

Many congregations and pastors wind up doing the same old things with the same people in the same old ways and thereby close the door on what new things the Spirit might want to do among them. The Spirit's inclination is to change people, not leave them in a rut.

How long do congregations today want to stay conformed to the sociological village pattern dominant in previous centuries?

THE LIMITS OF VILLAGE-CHURCH STYLE OF MINISTRY TODAY

We can recognize at least two practices today that were shaped by village-church ministry. One is the confirmation of fourteen-year-old children baptized as infants; the other is emphasis on the separation between clergy and laity.

Village churches baptize infants with the assumption the family will remain in the congregation and also with the congregation's intent to nurture their children into the faith that was professed for them by others. Confirmation became a graduation ritual by which the young adult personally affirms this faith. Such personal affirmation of baptismal faith happens typically at the end of the eighth grade, because until well into the twentieth century that was the end of formal school education. Teaching the church body's catechism was basic. Catechisms apply God's Word as knowledge and are aimed at heads, with the assumption hearts will follow.

There are sound theological reasons for baptizing infants, based on recognition that by grace God takes the initiative in his relationship to individuals. The real issue is fourteen-year-old confirmation. It made sense in the sheltered environment of a village, where all shared the same values and encountered few challenges to their faith.

Something more is needed, however, when children now go to schools that do not recognize the role of God in creation and where many students have lifestyles with very different values. Many church-raised children do not survive the transition with their entry-level faith intact. The head knowledge from confirmation needs to be strengthened with experiences that bring heart conviction. Fourteen-year-olds at least ought to be taught to expect challenge. It would be good for them to hear from predecessors a few years earlier who have worked through their doubts into deeper faith.

Going back to the years when the pastor was the only literate and educated person in the village, that old church culture made a clear distinction between clergy and laity, a distinction not found in Scriptures. The pastor personally does most of the ministry, joined in larger churches by others who are ordained or commissioned. The lay member's role is to support this ministry by making financial contributions and regularly attending church. For many, this is done with a sense of duty and habit. In a village, there is little room for recognizing spiritual gifts among laity.

Those stable village traditions worked well during population growth and migrations from the farm to the city in the early parts of the twentieth century in America. They persisted through the big-city migrations out to the suburbs in the 1950s and '60s, when there was a strong desire to join something and to replicate the churches they came from. But now, in the twenty-first century, it is time to recognize that what worked for traditional churches in earlier decades is not working well anymore in urbanized areas, as evidenced in the continued decline of congregations that still practice village traditions.

To put the issue differently, today the Holy Spirit does not seem to accomplish as much as he used to in the soil of congregations and ministries shaped by village culture. Such soil needs to be cultivated more creatively.

A friend told me a little story that illustrates the two cultures. She was talking to a sister who is a member of a city church with only twenty or so members in attendance. My friend relayed excitement over her congregation's project of serving free coffee and hot chocolate in the middle of the night to the people lined up to enter stores early for the Black Friday sales after Thanksgiving. The sister responded, "You're just trying to be different from us." Such a put-down is a classic example of village-church thinking that persists into the twenty-first century. Conformity is assumed. Without change, not many years of life remain for the sister's once-thriving congregation in the city.

LIFELONG GROWTH IN CHRISTLIKENESS WAS BASIC TO PAUL'S PERSPECTIVE

Village-church culture tends to assume that confirmed adults are mature Christians. If any more growth is expected, this would be in knowledge of the Bible, out of which should come greater faith and guidance for living. The village has little vocabulary to describe changes in heart condition brought by the Spirit and then the changed perceptions that follow. Emphasis is much more on comfort than on challenge.

Paul's understanding of maturity is quite different. No one ever reaches it. He tells the Ephesians that their local body of Christ should continue to be built up until all become mature, reaching the height of Christ's full stature (Ephesians 4:13 TEV). The Greek word translated as "mature" really means becoming all that you can be. In today's terms, it means self-actualization. Because the standard is Christlikeness, we will never reach full maturity as a Christian in this life.

Paul told the Corinthians, "We are being transformed into his likeness with ever-increasing glory, which comes from the Lord, who is the Spirit" (2 Corinthians 3:17, 18). In other words, the Spirit repeatedly changes us to become more Christlike and thereby to reflect more of God's glory. In all my years of Lutheran grade schools and high school, Lutheran colleges, and Lutheran seminary and in listening to thousands of sermons, I don't remember any special reference ever made to this passage. It does not fit the prevailing mind-set, which expects little from the Spirit and does not anticipate the big changes of personal transformation.

Note how Paul assumes ongoing growth in personality-changing fruit of the Spirit:

✓ We thank God because your faith is *growing more and more*, and the love every one of you has for each other is *increasing* (2 Thessalonians 1:3). (italics mine)

✓ May the Lord make your love *increase and overflow* for each other and for everyone else, just as ours does for you (1 Thessalonians 3: 12).

✓ All over the world this Gospel is *bearing fruit and growing*, just as it has been doing among you since the day you heard it and understood God's grace in all its truth (Colossians 1:6).

✓ Now he who supplies seed to the sower and bread for food will also supply and *increase* your store of seed and will *enlarge* the harvest of your righteousness (2 Corinthians 9: 10).

The apostle Peter, Paul's close colleague, shares the same assumption about continued growth in fruit of the Spirit. He writes, "For if you have these qualities in *increasing measure*, they will keep you from being ineffective and productive in your knowledge of our Lord Jesus Christ" (2 Peter 1:8). The qualities Peter specifies right before that passage are these: faith, goodness, knowledge, self-control, perseverance, godliness, brotherly kindness, and love. These same qualities are what Paul expected as the fruit of the Holy Spirit's influence.

In that passage, Peter adds the intriguing conviction that it is possible for Christians to be ineffective and unproductive. Literally, he says barren and unfruitful. Clearly, he expected growth in the fruit worked by the Holy Spirit, beyond whatever we can produce on our own. Christian faith brings eternal salvation, but it should also produce continued life-changing growth in this world.

CHRISTLIKENESS AND THE HOLY SPIRIT

What does Christ do in our lives today, and how does the Holy Spirit figure in? The second and the third persons of the Trinity are easily confused with each other, and it is much easier to develop a relationship with a son than with a blurry spirit.

The apostle John gives us the job description for each. The Spirit's job is to serve as God the Father's and the Son's advocate for what they want and offer in our lives (John 14:15, 25). The Greek word for this role is *parakletos*. "Comforter" is a weak translation. "Counselor" is better. Best is to think of an advocate, a lawyer, or agent who offers what someone else is ready to provide. The Holy Spirit advocates for the Father and the Son and makes accessible what they offer.

John, in his first letter, offers a parallel job description for the Son, Jesus Christ. Using the same word, *parakletos*, he writes, "If any body does sin, we have an advocate to the Father in our defense—Jesus Christ, the Righteous One" (1 John 2:1, 2). Thus, Jesus is our advocate, like a lawyer in God's courtroom, and the Holy Spirit is the Father's and Son's advocate to us in our daily lives.

Here is how Jesus described the Spirit's job: "I will ask the Father, and he will give you another advocate to be with you forever—the Spirit of truth. The world cannot accept him, because it neither sees him nor knows him. But you know him, for he lives with you and will be in you. I will not leave you as orphans" (John 14:15). Later, Jesus said, "When the Spirit of truth comes, he will guide you into all truth; he will tell you what is yet to come. He will not speak on his own; he will speak only what he hears. He will bring glory to me by taking from what is mine and making it known to you" (John 16:13).

The images of wind and fire were used for the Holy Spirit that first Pentecost. But for me, those images do not seem very personal. I find it is easier to think of the Spirit's advocacy in the form of that dove that came down from the sky to sit on Jesus' shoulder at his baptism. This image can replace the oblong blur that so many believers imagine the Holy Spirit to be. I have learned to picture him sitting on my shoulder throughout the day, whispering into my ear thoughts that would make me react in more Christlike ways to what is going on around me. The dove urges me to respond constructively and warns against hurtful ways. The same Spirit gives the ability to discern the differences.

For Paul, lifelong growth in Christlikeness is the best description of what Christian living is all about. We have four Gospels' worth of narratives about what Jesus was like, the values he held, the behaviors he showed, and the claims he made. Various descriptions of the process of growing more Christlike will be discussed in chapter 6.

In Paul's thinking, when we talk about life in Christ, we are at the same time talking about life in the Spirit. These are two ways of describing the same experience—two sides of the same coin. To become more Christlike is to be filled more by the Holy Spirit. As he tells the Corinthians, "You are righteous in the name of the Lord Jesus Christ and by the Spirit of our God" (1 Corinthians 6: 11).

In his book *Union with Christ*, Reformed theologian Lewis Smedes does the detailed study that shows their equivalence. Key passages are in note 27 at the end of this book.[27] They show that having the Spirit in us and having Christ in us are one and the same. We have life through Christ; we have life through the Holy Spirit. We are consecrated in Christ Jesus; we are consecrated in the Holy Spirit. We are told to live in Christ; we are told to walk in the Spirit. We are called into the fellowship of Christ; we are blessed with the fellowship of the Holy Spirit. Technically, the spirit of the ascended Christ is with us now as Holy Spirit.

Spiritual formation is a process of reaching higher and higher to the full stature of Christ (Ephesians 4:13). Do you want to become more like Christ? You can't do it on your own. Concentrate rather on receiving more from the Holy Spirit. With our own abilities and powers, we cannot change and move very far toward Christlikeness. But using those abilities and powers, we can cultivate the Holy Spirit's work in our hearts, and congregations can become better hosts of the Spirit.

GARDENER, BUILDER, SHEPHERD

Paul told the Corinthians they were God's garden as well as God's building (1 Corinthians 3:9). For him, the work of ministry is cultivating the land that presents itself in the people of a specific congregation, promoting lifelong growth in Christlikeness. Given his emphasis on different gifts of the Spirit, I think Paul envisioned a garden of many different plants, not a field with all the same crop. He also focused on a second image of joining and building church participants together as a temple in the Lord (Ephesians 2:21, 22).

Paul's gardener and builder self-images got lost over the centuries in favor of the shepherd image, which Paul himself does not use.

Consider: "You are God's garden." "I planted the seed, Apollos watered it, but God made it grow" (1 Corinthians 3:9, 6). After Paul calls the Corinthian congregation God's garden, he goes right on to say, "You are God's building. By the grace God has given me, I laid a foundation as an expert builder, and someone else is building on it." He expands the building image with this explanation to the Ephesians: "In Christ the whole building is joined together and rises to become a holy temple in the Lord. You are being built together to become a dwelling in which God lives by his Spirit (1 Corinthians 2:21–22).

When Paul laid a foundation for a congregation, he was not only teaching them the life-changing truths of what God offers in Jesus, the Christ, through his Holy Spirit, but he also was modeling how the Spirit works differently in individuals. He modeled how the leadership challenge is to build up and integrate growth-stimulating relationships among those who responded to the new gospel of grace he proclaimed. Get the foundation of grace-oriented, Spirit-inspired relationships right, and a lasting and fruitful local body of Christ will be easier to build up into a unique temple.

Your Perspective Compared to Paul's

Imagine you are a leader looking at two hundred worshipers gathered on Sunday morning. What do you see?

Using the gardener metaphor, do you recognize their *similarities* and view those people as a field with rows of, say, corn or soybeans? Or do you focus on their *differences* and see a garden with many kinds of plants at various stages in their growth? Some are still children. Are the grownups all about the same? To be sure, your job as leader is much easier if you see mostly the similarities and expect little beyond their participation and support. Are they mostly the same from year to year, or are you seeing change and growth in their character and relationships? Can you recall their individual stories of spiritual growth and journey that you have helped celebrate? Do you see spiritually healthy plants, or do too many show signs of failure to thrive.

Shift to the temple image. Are you seeing those gathered together on a Sunday morning as a one-room temple, or can you recognize a more complicated structure of many rooms under one roof? Are you focused mostly on maintaining this spiritual temple, doing the routine ministry tasks they expect? Or do you want to build it up into something different and better, even without growth in numbers? Is your ministry mostly encouraging and patching up what is there already? Or do you have in mind what *could be* there with a few renovation efforts, or by taking on several remodeling projects, or by adding on a few rooms for those with special interests and needs? We are not talking about constructing physical rooms but rather about building up the most Christlike fellowship of those who are gathered in all their diversity.

An inherent problem in congregational ministry is getting beyond the limitations of one-size-fits-all. It is the same message that all hear and usually the same worship format, as well as the same Bible classes. But the participants are not all the same size and don't give the same responses. Some are still beginners, and others think there is nothing more to learn. A few learn by reading, more by listening, and even more by discussion, while many others learn by doing. Some sense God's presence best in traditional rituals and symbols, others in acts of service, still others by involvement in their community, and some by growing in knowledge. Pastors themselves tend to focus on knowledge and often are surprised by how few others share such a passion for the Word. Indeed, while some few are passionate about their faith, many others are at best lukewarm.

DIFFERENT PATHWAYS FOR PERSONAL JOURNEYS WITH THE SPIRIT

The constant temptation in life with other Christians is to expect others to experience the work of the Holy Spirit in the same way you do. This is especially true for those in church bodies that emphasize their favorite gifting by the Spirit to speak in tongues or to give prophetic utterances. Paul would point out that it is up to God to determine which gift of the Holy Spirit he will give to whomever he chooses. It is crucial to avoid implying that those with different experiences are somehow second-class Christians.

The differences start all the way back with basic temperaments that people show from early age. It is one thing to know this in theory but something else to show the practical implications. Description and measurement became possible with the publication of the Myers-Briggs Type Indicator in 1972, which is now administered to two million people a year, mostly in corporate settings. The Myers-Briggs focuses on normal populations and emphasizes the value of naturally occurring differences.

One of the earliest applications of this indicator to prayer came with survey insights described by Charles Keating in *Who We Are Is How We Pray*.[28] That title would work as a heading for this section.

The Myers-Briggs asks questions that assess on which end of four different variables find yourself, and it yields sixteen combinations. The problem I found is that sixteen possible combinations are more than I can keep in mind and be able to move to practical application for participants. But the theory opens up a new understanding of why it is important to offer a variety of opportunities for experiencing God in ways suited to more than one temperament.

Gary Thomas offers a much better application in *Sacred Pathways: Discover Your Soul's Path to God*.[29] He narrows the options to nine that intuitively make sense and can be found in Scriptures. These are:

The *Naturalist*: Loving God Out-of-Doors. Finds a walk through the woods to be very conducive to prayer.

The *Sensate*: Loving God with the Senses. Wants to be lost in awe, beauty, and splendor of God.

The *Traditionalist*: Loving God through Ritual and Symbol. Likes structured worship with symbols and sacraments.

The *Ascetic*: Loving God in Solitude and Simplicity. Wants to be left alone in prayer.

The *Activist*: Loving God through Confrontation. Serves a God of justice, and church fills a need to recharge batteries.

The *Caregiver*: Loving God by Loving Others. Serves God by serving others.

The *Enthusiast*: Loving God with Mystery and Celebration. Wants to be inspired by joyful celebration.

The *Contemplative*: Loving God through Contemplation. Likes images of loving Father and Bridegroom.

The *Intellectual*: Loving God with the Mind. Drawn to explore basic issues in theology and church life.

This is not the place to go into a detailed exploration of these sacred pathways. That book is set up for you to do so on your own, with appropriate illustrations, identification of the characteristic temptations that come with each temperament, and a rating scale of six questions for each path, so you can identify which temperament seems most like you.

It should be no surprise that my temperament is the intellectual. I have many colleagues strongly oriented to ritual and sacraments. While I agree with the theology, I have grown more willing to admit that the sacraments have less resonance with me than it obviously has with them. Part of remaining an effective church and church body is to learn how to accommodate different temperaments.

THE VILLAGE CHURCH AND VERY LARGE CHURCHES TODAY

If a wide range of offerings is important for congregations in the future, then the future increasingly will be with very large congregations.

One legacy of the village is a one-pastor, small congregation with perhaps 100 to 150 in attendance. In a village the parish boundaries would provide a limited number of families within walking distance.

There is good research evidence that the future of Protestantism is toward mega-churches with attendance of one thousand or more. They continue to grow, while average congregations are in decline. Also, they have a larger proportion of younger generations.[30]

How does a congregation become a mega-church? My conclusion is that it happens under an unusual set of conditions, many of which are beyond the congregation's control. The key factor seems to be movement of the Holy Spirit. When the Spirit is blowing, the congregation then has to hurry to add buildings, parking, and staff to keep up with the growth. Like most things with the Spirit, his influence is easy to stop. In this case, it would be by not accommodating more people.

The congregation I serve has an attendance of about one thousand. We grew by 15–20 percent a year in the late '90s. We have plateaued since. An essential part of the growth about fifteen years ago was a feature article in the local newspaper about the new wave of contemporary worship. It featured our church, with a large photograph on the Sunday front page. Our attendance went up by two hundred in the following six months. No one can plan such media coverage. Somewhere in all that, the Holy Spirit was at work.

This chapter and the previous have addressed the biblical framework for recognizing the Spirit at work. Central is Paul's focus on spiritual gifts and the subset of fruit of the Spirit. He had the leadership self-confidence to recognize the Spirit-given diversity among those gathered in his congregations. He was willing as well to rely on the Spirit to produce growth in fruit, basic to living with differences. Both the diversity and lifelong growth were lost in the village-church setting of congregations over the centuries. Rediscovering Paul's framework for ministry can bring new effectiveness and excitement to congregational life.

PART III
How to Prepare for and Share Encounters with the Spirit

CHAPTER 5
Cultivate the Soil of Personal and Church Life

> Repent ... and you will receive the gift of the Holy Spirit
> —ACTS 2: 38

When my brothers and I spent summers on the Illinois farms of relatives, we saw that their major task in midsummer was to cultivate the soil between the rows of corn. The actual cultivator was a set of toe-like triangles that was lowered to about three inches below the surface and pushed along by the tractor, which would be outfitted for about six rows. It was a summer version of deeper plowing in the springtime to plant the seed. Summer cultivation worked the soil to dig up the weeds and let rainwater penetrate more readily to the roots of the corn stalk. Working the soil yielded a better harvest.

Use this image of cultivating the soil to picture the primary tasks of ministry. The seed to be planted and grow is God's Word. The harvest to look for is the gifts received from the Spirit in the form of energy to do ministry and also in the fruit of love and better relationships, as developed in chapter 3. From this primary harvest come greater passions to worship the Father in spirit as well as truth (John 4:24), to absorb God's Word, and to reach out to others with the gospel and in service. The point here is that harvest will be greater when the soil is periodically broken up—that is, cultivated.

Working the soil is implied in the first parable Jesus told, the parable of the sower and the seed. He used it to show how his ministry was all about initiating the kingdom of God in this world. Luther explains that the kingdom of God comes to us when the Father gives us his Holy Spirit, so that by his grace we believe his Word and live a godly life. The parable of the sower identifies four kinds of soil. The seeds will not bear much fruit when they land on a hard path, or rocky soil, or among weeds. The seeds that land on good soil yield a crop a hundred times greater than what is planted.

The leadership challenge is to improve the hard, rocky, and weedy soil as much as possible. Purposely cultivating the soil is important, both in the lives of individual Christians and in their lives together as a congregation.

PERSONAL PREPARATION FOR THE SPIRIT

Christian tradition rightly recognizes that the basic preparation for any encounter with God is repentance. Each needs to review and establish his or her relationship right up front. Basically, this means acknowledging "I am sorry" for how I messed up. I confess the ways I have been less Christlike than I should and want to be.

The apostle Peter ended his Pentecost proclamation with the call to repent and the promise, "And you will receive the gift of the Holy Spirit" (Acts 2: 38).

The Bible offers at least three images for how to approach God in repentance. One is the parable of the Pharisee and the publican (Luke 18:9-14). This religious superman reviewed all the ways he was a good man, as if that would win him special favor with God. The publican looked down, beat his breast, and confessed, "God, have mercy on me, a sinner." The punch line is that those who humble themselves will be looked upon favorably by God.

A second similar image is in James's letter when he states God's view succinctly: "God opposes the proud but gives grace to the humble" (James 4:6). This crisp proverb sets the context for the other gospel in a nutshell about how God in his grace sent his Son, that whoever believes in him will have eternal life (John 3:16). The basic preparation for encountering God is to humble oneself. Another way to state this is that when you are full of yourself, like the Pharisee, there is no room for the Holy Spirit to maneuver in your heart and soul. You first have to reduce the amount of yourself.

The third image is given by Isaiah when he sees the majesty of the Lord, seated on his throne as the seraphs sang "Holy, holy, holy." Their voices shook the temple doorposts, and the temple was filled with smoke. The only thing a human can say in the presence of such majesty is, "Woe is me! I am ruined! For I am a man of unclean lips" (Isaiah 6:5). Would that we could keep this image of God's majesty before us all the time. But over time, we humans tend to cut God down to our size and let the Pharisee in us slip into our thinking.

In chapter 2, I made reference to Jonathan Edwards's description of reliable characteristics of an encounter with the Spirit. He also offered a description of his own feelings at his personal second awakening: "I had great sense of humility, brokenness of heart and poverty of my soul. My heart panted after this, to lie low before God, and in the dust, that I might be nothing and that God might be all; that I might become as a little child."[31]

In his special encounter with the Spirit, Edwards wanted to "become as a little child." The mystery of God's kingdom is such that not only will it include children but indeed, as Jesus explained, it requires being like a child (Luke 18:17). Spiritual birth is as radically passive as physical birth; the chief actor is God, through his Holy Spirit. Our preparation is to humble ourselves and to seek his mercy. This is true repentance

Personal Hard Paths, Rocks, and Weeds

What are the hard paths, the rocks, and the weeds in our personal spiritual lives? The *hard paths* could be the superficial routines we insist on following that keep us focused on other things, like sport, job, success, money, and even family. The seeds of the kingdom of God cannot even take root because there is no room in our busyness.

The *rocks* could well be our routines that make us feel religious without being drawn closer to God. God's kingdom occasionally breaks through with short roots. But the roots cannot go deep, because we like our comfortable life and resist change.

The *weeds* could well be familiar distractions that we let choke out continued growth in our personal kingdom within. Weeds would be whatever keeps us from regular intake of God's Word through which the Holy Spirit works on our self-perceptions. Weeds could be whatever we let keep us from regular interaction with other Christians who can help us discern God's will in the circumstances we face.

SOIL-RELATED MINISTRIES IN CONGREGATIONAL LIFE

Eugene Peterson, translator of *The Message* version of the Bible, offers a vivid description of a congregation as topsoil for pastoral leadership.

> Congregation is the topsoil in pastoral work. This is the material substance in which all the Spirit's work takes place—these people, assembled in worship, dispersed in blessing. They are so ordinary, so unobtrusively there; it is easy to take them for granted.

> But this is the field of pastoral work, just as it is, teeming with energy, nutrients, mixing death and life. I cannot manufacture it, but I can protect it. I can nourish it. I can refrain from polluting or violating it. But mostly, like the farmer with his topsoil, I must respect and honor and reverence

it, be in awe before the vast mysteries contained in its unassuming ordinariness.[32]

Envision the hard top soil in a church as reliance on routines and traditions that offer little opportunity to make things new, which is the Spirit's specialty. The rocks might be hearts hardened by past conflicts and rigid dogmatism, in need of the Spirit to soften them. The weeds might be activities in a congregation that distract from the church's spiritual mission of helping God's kingdom come among those gathered through the Spirit's work.

My reaction to the three kinds of soil that yield low harvest is shaped by the pragmatic instinct of a church leader. Let's fix it. Let's improve the soil. While we cannot manage the Holy Spirit, we can work on changing the soil present in a congregation's life together. We can break up surfaces hardened by unchanging routines. We can add loose soil between the rocks. We can pull weeds out of our church life. Call these three steps part of skillfully cultivating the top soil of church life.

Breaking Up Hard Surfaces

Any congregation that meets regularly over the years develops routines and traditions for how they worship, learn, serve, and work together. Over time, the surfaces of these structures become hardened and closed to new expectations of what the Spirit can do in their midst. The soil will better host the Spirit's work when those routine expectations are frequently unsettled by new and different ways of sharing the gospel within a congregation. Then more water of the Word can seep deeper into the soil of this church's life together. Then the Spirit can work more effectively on the roots of God's special kingdom, wanting to grow in the heart of individual believers. When the routines and traditions of a congregation become hardened to new expectations, then that church lives mostly on memory, without fresh energy. Over time, the old spiritual energy runs out.

Increasingly, new definitions of the key words "spiritual" and "religious" are emerging to describe what is happening in declining denominations. According to historian Robert Fuller:

> The word *spiritual* gradually came to be associated with the private realm of thought and experience, while the word *religious* came to be connected with the public realm of membership in religious institutions, participation in formal ritual and adherence to official denominational doctrines ... "Spirituality" is taken as a positive term, whereas "religious" is often negative.[33]

For many observers, "religion" has become the villain in spiritual life. Note these titles of recent books: *Christianity without Religion, God without Religion,* and *Jesus without Religion.*[34] In the present context, religion is what happens when church routines and traditions have become hardened surfaces, with little new spiritual energy. Having spent my entire career serving institutions, I cannot join that bandwagon of casting off external forms. But as an insider, I will observe that the routines and structures of many traditional churches are no longer in sync with our changing times. Traditional Christian "religion" needs to change its ways in order to become more "spiritual" for newer generations.

Dealing with Rocks

In Jesus' parable of the sower, the second place where seed landed was on rocky ground, where there was little soil. "The seeds soon sprouted, because the soil wasn't deep. But when the sun came up, it burned the young plants; and because the roots had not grown deep enough, the plants soon dried up" (Mark 4:3–8 TEV).

Practically speaking, there are only two ways to deal with rocky ground if you want something to grow there: get rid of the rocks, or add soil.

But first, define rocky ground in a congregation. I take this to be participants who remain very superficial in their interactions with God. They get enthused for a while by interaction with others in worshiping God or serving others, but they soon settle back into old ways of avoiding the Word and staying distant from the Spirit. The roots of God's kingdom in their hearts cannot go very deep. Pressures of life will dry up those roots, and these people fade away from the Spirit's reach. Or their hardened hearts resist the Spirit's continued work through the Word, and further growth of God's plant in them is stunted. Their church life becomes a comforting routine and tradition of their religious—rather than spiritual—life.

"Throw these rocks out" is one response. The church is only for true believers, defined by various criteria. Pentecostals reserve church membership only for those who have experienced the second baptism of the Spirit by speaking in tongues. Or the congregation is only for those who have experienced a "true" conversion, as expected in many Evangelical churches.

But there is wisdom in the parable Jesus told right after explaining the seed and soils. While it is directed to weedy soil, it applies to rocky soil as well. When weeds appeared, servants asked the owner whether they should pull them out. The answer was no, because they might pull out some of the wheat along with them. Sort it out later. So, too, leave the rocks where they are. At least while such are present in a church, the Holy Spirit has additional opportunities to work on softening their hearts.

The apostle Paul explained that just the confession of Jesus as Lord is work done by the Spirit. That is sufficient for eternal salvation. His theology was all about the Spiritual growth that comes afterwards. Much to the disappointment of many Evangelicals, traditional churches of the Reformation believe that just a head-knowledge confession that Jesus is the Christ is sufficient for eternal salvation and for participation in a Christian congregation. The pastoral leadership challenge is to foster ongoing growth of God's inward reign through the work of the Holy Spirit.

We need to recognize that such growth in discipleship was not much in mind for the Reformers who, as they focused on eternity, wanted to get the doctrine right and assumed that hearts would follow heads.

Add More Soil

So don't throw out the rocks. Add soil for deeper roots.

Adding more soil can amount to increasing the number of stories about how the Spirit impacts lives today, especially among existing members. More stories come through carefully cultivating the congregational "Holy Spirit culture" that Harold Ellens envisioned, as noted in chapter 1. He commented on the excitement of living life, always consciously anticipating how the Holy Spirit of God will show up around the next corner.

One story Ellens tells concerns a friend of his waiting in the checkout line at a grocery store.

> The lady ahead of her was struggling with her glasses, checkbook, pen, and paraphernalia. As she struggled, she remarked to the clerk that she was upset and confused because her mother was dying. My friend spontaneously expressed concern about how hard that can be. This led to an extended conversation, in which she was able to share the burden of that stranger and communicate to her the consolations that my friend experienced in sailing her life close to the wind of the spirit, so to speak. This struck a responsive chord in the stranger's soul, and the upshot of the event was a great sense of strength and renewal for both persons.[35]

Ellens stresses the importance of naming those moments as events "of the spirit" and then of sharing them with others so that they become a conscious culture of the Holy Spirit and are not forgotten. He proposes that developing such a culture means doing the following:

✓ Expect to experience the presence of God's Spirit in tangible ways regularly.

✓ Notice those manifestations of God's Spirit in ordinary and extraordinary moments and events.

✓ Name those moments as "of the Spirit."

✓ Explain those moments to each other and thus raise the consciousness level of all.

✓ Continually recall together that those moments have happened and continue to happen.

✓ Come to think of ourselves as the body of Christ, constantly made lively by that Spirit of God, living in the expectation of more experiences of the Spirit's presence to us in tangible ways.[36]

Pulling Weeds from Church Life

Let God decide whether an individual participant is a weed. The weeds to pull out of the soil of church life are those that creep into the structures that leaders develop to shape and protect the interactions of their primary spiritual fellowship.

Weeds are anything that distracts from the primary nature and mission of the fellowship gathered together as believers. Examples could be fund-raisers, renting out facilities, having meetings without invoking God's presence, and maybe even having special "fellowship" events. Our goal at the church I serve is to "make and grow disciples." In practical terms, this means, don't waste leadership or congregational time or energy on anything not directly related to making and growing disciples. The rest is weeds.

In the first chapter, I presented the challenge to give fellowship of the Spirit priority over church organization. Organizing gets formalized with such techniques as constitutions, carefully crafted goals, written job descriptions and assignments, and designated work relationships. Such management practices have become a key part of our current American culture. This is a good news/bad news development for churches. The good news comes with skillful pastoral leadership that keeps the formal structure focused on the primary fellowship.

The bad news is when organizational techniques squeeze out recognition and reliance on the Spirit's often spontaneous influence on the hearts and motivations of the believer. Then such a congregation begins to look and act like any other social organization. Then it begins to resemble the many community clubs that are in rapid decline in American society today, offering opportunities for "involvement" without special motivation by the Spirit. Such congregations are likely to find themselves withering away to their final end sooner or later. While some may prolong life by renting out their facilities for income, this approach is likely to choke out the Spirit's influence even more.

Developing Spirit-Led Community

James W. Jones, professor of religion at Rutgers University, reflected on spontaneous fellowships that emerged in the American youth counterculture movement of the 1960s, when communes of twentysomethings dropped out to live together "to realize one's potential, to get themselves together." He participated in some and shared his observations as a Christian.

Most of the participants he saw were searchers in "a circle of empty vessel, each waiting to be filled. Since every vessel is empty, no one has anything to pour into the gaping containers." Most of those communes got into trouble and fell apart after a few months or a year. He notes that in America, only religious communes have survived any length of time. They have something to share with others.

Jones observed, "We on our own cannot create community no matter how hard we try. Community flows from a shared experience, an experience that fills individual vessels so they have something to pour out into the other vessels. This experience is the work of the Holy Spirit."

Many who could not live communally in small settings felt guilty about their failure. Jones counseled, "They shouldn't have; koinonia is a gift of the Spirit, not a natural human possibility. The experience of koinonia is something given us, not something we create. Christian community is not built by building Christian community. It is the side result of doing something else, like following the lead of the Spirit.¹⁷

The original Christian church of Acts 2 was a commune. "Selling their possessions and goods, they gave to any one as he had need." But very quickly, that spontaneous fellowship had to get structured and administered. It started with appointment of Stephen and six others to oversee food distribution. Some thirty years later, Paul had to increase the formal organization by giving to Timothy written job descriptions for leaders and also supplying welfare-like rules about which widows qualified (1 Timothy 3; 5). Even at the very beginning there was no lasting alternative to developing structure and institutionalizing some relationships.

To use the now popular distinction between "spiritual" and "religion," pure spiritual fellowship will not last long without taking on some external forms now derided as just "religion." The challenge for the leaders of these external structures is to keep their focus on the primary spiritual fellowship that gives life to whatever forms are developed.

As our American culture gets increasingly used to administered relationships, a church's organization needs more pastoral supervision so the focus stays on the ways of the Holy Spirit. In management terms, the senior pastor is the chief spiritual officer (CSO) and often will need to add the role of chief executive officer (CEO).

A CALL TO CHURCH REPENTANCE

Part of cultivating the soil of church life is to hear Peter's call to those hearers gathered on the first Pentecost to *"repent and be baptized."*

An annual day of congregational repentance was part of the soil of good church culture that was left behind years ago in my church body. It was not just individual repentance but repentance by the whole congregation.

What that could be is shown in excerpts from the sermon by Pastor C. F. W. Walther in 1870, thirty-one years after the beginning of Trinity Lutheran in St. Louis. They had much to be thankful for—they had grown from few to many and from a poor church to a wealthy one with a large sanctuary and school. Yet "We are no longer what we were. Today should be a call to repentance." Whether they have truly gone forward or backward "hinges on how things stand, first, in respect to faith in God and, second, in respect to love to the neighbor. For just as only faith and love make a Christian into a genuine Christian, so these two parts alone make a congregation into a genuine congregation."

To this pastor, this congregation had gone backwards. With respect to faith in God, "Instead of an eager digging for the gold of the truth in Holy Scriptures and in other good books, isn't there now among most of our members a running and rushing after earthy riches, after big business deals."

With respect to neighborly love, whereas they were once like a family, now

do not many all too often manifest indifference, yes, coldness over against those they know are brothers and members of the congregation? Is it not only too evident that, on the part of many, a respectable child of the world is regarded more worthily and highly than a brother or sister? Has not the zeal to win souls practically died out among us? Has not brotherly admonition almost entirely vanished? Does not "backbiting and evil speaking" against brothers and sisters rule in almost all our meetings?

Oh, let us therefore today above all appear before the holy God as a fallen congregation in genuine contrition and repentance ... Oh, if today we return to God repentant and believing, this day will be the day of the rebirth of our congregation and a time of new visitation of God's grace and new, greater blessings will dawn up her.[38]

CHAPTER 6
Share Stories of Personal Spiritual Journey

Since we live by the Spirit, let us
keep in step with the Spirit.
—GALATIANS 5:25

The first name given to Christians was People on the Way, on a journey. The Greek word for journey shows up in English when we talk about the dashboard *odo*-meter in an automobile. This measures the miles that have been driven. It is really a record of journeys taken with that car.

My current Honda has taken me on eighty-five thousand miles of journey. These are a blur, since they are mostly to and from the church office, on errands around Cleveland, and visiting children. The odometer on my 1981 Pontiac station wagon, however, told a very different story. It took the family on two cross-country moves and six summers of family vacation all around the West, including six scenic national parks. The most special of the Pontiac's journey were family experiences while the children were in grade school and high school—camping in the Northwest, dodging forest fires in Yellowstone, seeing a bull fight in Mexico, Mom reading to the children in the car for hours, kids squabbling over who gets the "way back" in the station wagon.

We like to retell stories of those journeys, like spending a whole night sleeping in the station wagon because I did not stop early enough to find an available motel room. It rained most of the night so we could not open the windows much. Biffy, our dog, was this story's star—or villain—because he passed a lot of gas that night.

To tell one's spiritual journey is simply to recall personal memories from years of living in Christ. Where did it start—as a child or as an adult? Some Christians have in focus their conversion experience at a specific time and place. Others always knew they were Christians from childhood on. More important than where the journey started is where a believer is right now. What were some of the high points and then also the low points? Sometimes the low points are necessary to get to the "mountaintop" experiences.

"Spiritual journey" is a wonderful concept in the conversations of many Christians today. Personal stories of life with the Spirit are somewhat foreign to traditional church cultures, which tend to have a more static outlook on the Christian life, as if little of personal spiritual significance happens through their adult lives.

When Paul first saw People on the Way (Acts 9:3), he recognized they were going someplace and not just to heaven. They were dangerous, because theirs was a journey different from Jewish tradition. Years later, he described them as on the way to becoming more mature people, "reaching together to the very height of Christ's full stature" (Ephesians 4:13). He urged them to go their way "in step with the Spirit." Over time, an adult Christian should become a different person from when she or he first knowingly affirmed his or her faith.

Faith journeys are really stories of growth through encounters with the Holy Spirit. One of the many stories Paul could tell of his expanding ministry was encountering the Spirit's work in his release from prison (Philippians 1: 19). Most congregations have stories to tell of their growth as they were being built together to become a dwelling in which God encountered them through his Spirit (Ephesians 2: 22).

Paul would say that if you are talking about spiritual journeys, and you are not looking for the Holy Spirit, then recognize that you are not talking about Christian spirituality.

HAVING MORE OR LESS OF THE SPIRIT AT ANY ONE TIME

Luke uses the unique and helpful phrase "full of the Holy Spirit," which he then couples with a specific characteristic to describe what that fullness brought. In Luke's gospel, Elizabeth was full of the Holy Spirit and *rejoiced* about her blessedness. Zechariah was full of the Spirit and *prophesized*. In Acts, the apostles chose the seven helpers, whom they recognized as full of the Holy Spirit and *wisdom*. In one passage, Stephen was full of the Holy Spirit and *faith*. Peter and John were full of the Holy Spirit and proclaimed *boldly*. Barnabas was full of the Holy Spirit and *faith*.

These people of God had the Spirit with them always but occasionally more so at a specific time and place. Then they had the Spirit to a fuller degree that gave them unusual wisdom, faith, power, or boldness. They certainly also would have had times when they had less of the Spirit at work in them.

The description of being full of the Holy Spirit at a certain time offers the image of each believer as a vessel or pot into which God pours his Spirit. Indeed, Paul explicitly used that image when explaining to the Corinthians, "We have this treasure [the gospel] in jars of clay" (2 Corinthians 4:7). To Titus, he used the vivid image of the Spirit being poured out upon us (2 Corinthians 2:6).

This image gets even better when we picture the vessel as having a hole in it. This hole in our personal pot is the sinful nature that remains with even the best of Christians. Resistance to the Spirit by our remaining old nature amounts to a hole, out of which the Spirit leaks, sometimes to the point that the vessel is almost empty.

Even better is to add to this image the picture of the jar overflowing with what is poured into it. One of Paul's favorite words is usually translated as overflowing or excelling or abundant. Thus, he tells the Romans about God's overflowing provision of grace (Romans 5:5). He encourages the troubled Corinthians to excel (rise even more) in spiritual gifts that build up the church (1 Corinthians 14:12). In nine other places, he couples the word with one or the other fruit of the Spirit, such as overflowing love (three times), overflowing joy (two times), overflowing thanksgiving, and overflowing wisdom and understanding. These forms of overflowing add depth to the psalmist's praise, "My cup overflows." This word for overflowing is the one Jesus used when explained how he came that they might have the abundant life—life overflowing (John 10:10).

What was Paul's major objective for the believers he was leading? He wanted primarily that they be filled by the Holy Spirit to the point of having so much of the Spirit that the Spirit's gifts and fruit overflow in their lives of abundance.

DESCRIPTIONS OF THE JOURNEY

The all-time favorite spiritual journey story is *The Pilgrim's Progress*, written in 1678 by John Bunyan and translated into two hundred languages. The pilgrim is a man named Christian and his wife, Christiana. Each has a separate journey on the way to the Celestial City. Many characters try to lure them off the right path. Others help them on the way. The tempters include Formalist, Hypocrisy, Timorous, Mistrust, Ignorance, and Giant Despair. The helpers have names like Good Will, Prudence, Faithful, Hopeful, and Old Honest. On the way, they have to pass through places like the Slough of Despond and the Valley of the Shadow of Death.

Recall Paul's examples of fruit of the Holy Spirit, like love, joy, peace, hope, faithfulness, and self-control. The pilgrim's helpers represent those characteristics. We, in turn, are invited to take those roles in helping others on their way. The tempters are their opposite. John Bunyan knew well that a believer's spiritual journey is shaped by the ups of growing in the fruit granted through the Holy Spirit and by the downs of being distracted from them.

One helpful description of the journey is offered by Willow Creek researchers in their report, *Reveal*.[39] They divide the journey into four stages: 1) Exploring Christianity, 2) Growing in Christ, 3) Close to Christ, and 4) Christ-Centered. These four stages, in turn, yield what they call three movements for a believer's spiritual journey. The first movement is from Exploring Christianity to Growing in Christ. The second movement is from Growing in Christ to Close to Christ. The third is from Close to Christ to Christ-Centered. The questionnaire results give characteristic behaviors and attitudes that accompany each movement.

These researchers wisely refrained from picking any one movement to call "conversion." In truth, a much better word is to describe each movement as an "awakening." Something happened that drew the participant closer to Christ. For every participant, these awakenings will be unique to his or her personal journey. It would be fascinating to hear each journey story. The variety of circumstances and influences would make abundantly clear that in church life, there is no "one size fits all." An interesting follow-up to that research would be to interview respondents to hear their stories of what happened to them in those movements of the Spirit.

One of my favorite descriptions of the journey is by Janet Hagberg and Robert Guelich in their book *The Critical Journey: Stages in the Life of Faith*. For them, stage 1 is recognition of God. Stage 2 is learning the life of discipleship. Stage 3 is the productive life, where most church professionals are included. Stage 4 is the very important journey inward. Getting to this point almost always involves "hitting the Wall" or an obstacle they cannot overcome with their ordinary efforts and skills. They try everything to scale it, circumvent it, burrow under it, go over it, or simply ignore it, but the Wall remains. The authors explain, "The Wall represents our will meeting God's will face-to-face and our discovering anew whether we are willing to surrender."[40]

The Wall could be a failed marriage, or lengthy unemployment, or very serious illness. The key is to learn to give up dependence on self and to surrender to God's loving providence. Then the Spirit's refreshing fruit of love, joy, peace, and hope can come to greater expression.

The biggest awakening of my personal spiritual journey came in February 1992, when I was recovering from an acute viral infection. Serious illness is a good time for the Holy Spirit to do his work. I was home, brooding about what was, among other things, the apparent failure of our biggest church plant outreach. The previous October, we had made our major effort, according to a program called "The Phone's for You." We had called every phone number in the target three suburbs to invite people to a special worship service. The big event was in November. But by February, there was no visible impact on attendance. Now what? In my brooding, I was a failure and probably would have to find ministry somewhere else. This was embarrassing for someone with high visibility in the Church Growth movement. Public failure is a great time for the Spirit to do his work.

I had hit the Wall. I was doing my part. Why wasn't God doing his part? Over several weeks, the Spirit worked on my heart until I came to a peace-giving acceptance: *So be it, even if I have to sell the house.* Having built several, I found the prospect of letting go of this new house to be the hardest part. After surrender came new energy and resolve. A year later, we found and remodeled a building in a park-like setting that became our church home. It made part of the foundation I left behind.

STRUGGLE

Meditation, prayer, and struggle—*meditatio, oratio,* and *tentatio* in Latin—was Martin Luther's prescription for the training of ministers. It is a good formula for the spiritual growth of any Christian. The third ingredient, struggle, is key to turning head knowledge into heartfelt conviction. Christian faith often stays superficial until it gets tested by some circumstance in which a believer's life does not go as expected, and his or her self-concept of life with God is shaken. The *tentatio* of spiritual life can result in a heartfelt experience that brings new intellectual insights. But many do not recover. They walk away from their superficial faith and look for some other approach to finding meaning. They are more likely to rebound in faith when they have stronger Christians around them who can interpret what is happening. Doing so is a fundamental purpose for the fellowship of Christians that is basic to church.

Struggle cannot be taught. It happens one by one through personal response to unique circumstances. But we can observe what it is like in others and learn how God worked it out their lives. It is the personal struggle of a "before" condition that sets up the compelling "after" story of a movement to greater convictional faith. Such stories are worth telling and hearing. This is more likely to happen when the story fits into a category and has a special vocabulary to describe what happened. Then, this transition to deeper faith can be celebrated with others. The story can give hope to others that the Spirit may help them grow too.

A pastor colleague of mine told a sad story that happened in his internship year, when he accompanied the pastor on a hospital visit. The woman patient talked about how she was so angry with God about her condition. The pastor said, "No, you are not" and proceeded to tell her why she should never be angry with God. What a squandered opportunity for spiritual growth. Such thinking is pure village culture, where the need to keep up appearances of faithfulness stifles struggle and therefore misses opportunities for growth.

REACHING STAGE 4 FAITH

A young staff member commented on "when I became a Christian in college." This intrigued me, because I knew she had been baptized as an infant, gone to Sunday school, had been confirmed, and was much involved in youth activities in her church. I challenged how she could say "when I became a Christian in college." She acknowledged that, yes, she knew she was a Christian before then, but her faith took on new meaning through involvement with a campus ministry. Those in that ministry had taught her the phrase.

To my way of reckoning, she had experienced an awakening. More specifically, she had moved from stage 3 of faith development to stage 4. Either way, God was at work in her life, and this high point in her spiritual journey was cause for celebration. May she have more awakenings in the years to come.

These stages of faith come from highly regarded developmental psychologist James Fowler. He posits that faith, rather than belief or religion, is the most fundamental category in the human quest for relation to transcendence. Fowler is a professor of theology and a Methodist minister.[41] His language is very academic. I prefer descriptions of the stages offered by theologian Thomas Droege and will use his titles for the first four of Fowler's six-stage framework to Christian faith development.[42] Consider these stages:

Stage 1. "God's just like my mommy and daddy"—the literalism characteristic of the preschooler.

Stage 2. "What's fair is fair!"—characteristic of a child seeing God as a stern law-giver.

Stage 2 remains the level of many adults whose approach to life is that you get from God what you earn. This leaves the uncertainty about the final judgment and whether your good deeds outweigh your sins. I have encountered many Christians who had known about God's grace all their lives but never quite caught the significance of his love and forgiveness for daily living. Knowledge alone does not always convert into a heart on which the Spirit has had much impact. Culture usually trumps preaching, and the routines of a village-church culture can leave personal faith unexamined in stage 2.

Stage 3. "I believe what the church believes"—characteristic of a teen's interpretation of faith and story, as taught by authority figures.

Stage 3 is typically at child-confirmation level. It is a faith taught by authority figures. At this stage, believers tend to have a hard time seeing outside their box and don't recognize that they are "inside" a belief system. It is unrealistic to expect a mature faith from fourteen-year-olds.

Stage 4. "As I see it, God is ..."—characteristic of young adults who form their own opinions on the way life is to be lived and how God acts in the world.

It is in stage 4 where knowledge turns into heartfelt conviction. This is a tough stage, often begun in young adulthood, when people start seeing outside the box and realize that there are other "boxes" of alternate values and understandings among those around them. They begin to critically examine their beliefs on their own and come to their own convictions. For many, this is new appreciation for the Christian faith in which they were nurtured.

When struggling between stage 3 and stage 4, many youth appear to fall away, leaving others shaking their heads at this loss. This can be village thinking. A hundred years ago, few young adults in a village ran into challenges to their faith. They accepted it and lived accordingly. In today's social culture, Christian teens are surrounded daily with peers who live by other values and even mock those who go to church. The challenge now is to move beyond village culture. Adopting a vocabulary for struggle and the possibility of recovery is a very wise move for traditional churches.

Being given and raised in an identity by parents and church is good, but choosing that identity after struggle is even better for growth in faith and discipleship. Recognizing and encouraging such a choice involves a different approach to ministry.

RECOGNIZING A TRANSFORMING EXPERIENCE

About 4:30 p.m. on Saturday, September 2, 1970, James Loder, his wife, and two daughters were on a New York highway, heading north to Canada in their camper. They spotted a middle-aged woman standing near an Oldsmobile with a flat tire and pulled off the road to help. Loder was trying to position the jack and had his head under the front of the car, looking for where he should place it, when a car driven by a man asleep at the wheel rammed the back of Olds and pushed it fifteen feet forward and into the back of the camper, with James dragged along with it. Trapped, with the front of the Olds on his chest, he called for help. Injuries included broken ribs, a punctured lung, skin scrapes from head to foot, and the tip of his thumb torn off. His wife, a slight woman, tried to help by lifting up on the bumper and was then surprised to see that the car lifted off her husband. She broke a vertebra in the effort.

Loder reports, "As I roused myself from under the car, a steady surge of life was rushing through me, carrying with it two solid assurances. First, I knew how deeply I felt love for those around me. The second assurance was that this disaster had a purpose. I never felt more conscious of the life that poured through me, nor more aware that this life was not my own."[43]

At that time, James Loder was a junior faculty member of Princeton Theological Seminary, where he went on to become professor of the Philosophy of Christian Education. Much of his academic career was devoted to understanding what happened in what he calls a "transforming moment" and how such moments emerge in the lives of many others. He calls it a "convicting experience." It was an encounter with the supernatural. It was an awakening of a very special kind, not granted to all.

THEOLOGICAL REPRESSION

One of Loder's discoveries is a survey result, showing that about 80 percent of Presbyterian clergy and half of their lay constituency have had some such experience, yet seldom are these talked about. Loder calls this situation a "theological repression."

Theological repression is a good term for what happens in a church culture that is not open to God's supernatural interventions. Such culture has little room for recognizing the Holy Spirit's interventions in bringing any special motivation for ministry and in producing character-changing extraordinary fruit. In such a culture, the Spirit part of the Trinity seems only partially known.

Gordon D. Fee, the foremost New Testament expert today on the Holy Spirit in the letters of Paul, tells about a student who said to him, "God the Father I understand, Christ the Son I know, but the Holy Spirit is a gray, oblong blur." Fee goes on to observe that for many church communities, the Spirit is kept in the creed, lest he become a vital—and perhaps threatening—part of the church's ongoing life. Thus, in belief, Protestants maintain their Trinitarianism, but in practice, many are thorough-going binitarians.[44]

To continue to ignore the third person is one reaction, in effect repressing what cannot be explained. A better response is to recognize, seek understanding, and adjust one's view of God accordingly. We can learn to wait upon the Spirit, who can be full of surprises.

"Transformation" has become a buzzword in corporate as well as church cultures. Transformations are good. They represent changes that result in better performance for organizations and better living for individuals.

But true transformations are seldom. The word itself comes from Latin, meaning to change forms. The Greek version we know as *metamorphosis*— what parents teach children about caterpillars that turn into butterflies. This is a thorough change. Personal transformations are usually dramatic and very memorable. They are quite different from step-by-step transitions. Most religious experiences are somewhere in between. These are still important to share. But transformational awakenings are especially important.

Reflections on a Transforming Moment

We return to James Lober and his September 2, 1970, accident. Reflecting on it, he observes, "I never felt more conscious of the life that poured through me, nor more aware that this life was not my own."

He begins *The Transforming Moment* with his description of the accident and how this incident led him to a "convictional knowledge" of who he is, in relation to God, as experienced in a close brush with death. It was conviction beyond reason. Such stories are often told as an experience of conversion. Understanding this experience is important in order to avoid "an anti-intellectual rush of enthusiastic clichés." Such emotional enthusiasms are a symptom that theology has not been able "to supply understanding, comprehension and an adequate language for what takes place in these convicting moments of transformation."[45]

Here are several more generalizations Loder offers about such transforming experiences:

✓ No one can know or comprehend the central meaning of a convicting experience from a standpoint outside of it. It is intensely personal.

✓ The validation of a word from God is uniformly established by God's initiative, not by generally recognized human procedures.

✓ A claim to having heard God's word may be falsified by human means but is finally and ultimately validated by God.

✓ Knowing—generally and convictionally—is first, foremost, and fundamentally an event. At the center is a nonrational intrusion of a convincing insight.[46] I would add the comment that such an *event* is really an *encounter* with Jesus Christ, like Paul had on the road to Damascus.

STORIES OF SPIRIT AND MEMORY

There is growing recognition that communicating the gospel is best done by telling stories. This is what Jesus did, and this is what the four Gospels do. The apostle Paul recognized that each believer in Corinth could tell a story of before and after his encounter with Christ. "You show that you are a letter from Christ, the result of our ministry, written not with ink but with the Spirit of the living God, not on tablets of stone but on tablets of human hearts" (2 Corinthians 3:3).

Good theory backs up this observation about the power of stories. It comes from John Shea, a master storyteller as well as a theologian especially popular in Roman Catholic circles. He is also good at explaining the significance of storytelling for spirituality in the context of church.

Here are some highlights from his book, *An Experience Named Spirit: Spirituality and Storytelling*. Shea's two main concepts are Spirit and Memory.

Spirit is the Holy Spirit at work in so many lives and circumstances. Story is one of the primal expressions of the experience named Spirit, and Christian faith regularly retells its sacred stories. The great hope of every retelling is that the tale will powerfully intersect the life of the hearers, so they will experience in some way the reality of Spirit.[47]

Memory is accumulation of remembered rituals, espoused beliefs and theologies, and enacted values and behaviors that are shared. Christians are people of Spirit and Memory, whose souls are their living relationship with God, which is activated by the experience named Spirit. Memories are stockpiled as generation succeeds generation, and they are constantly in need of reform in order to be faithful to the living God at work in new generations. Traces of this Memory, like songs, worship, and buildings, have many different and very important functions but only one ultimate purpose. They are expressions of the experience named Spirit and are meant to facilitate that experience for all who currently come into contact with the gospel.

The basic question is, which data of personal experience are of religious significance? Said differently, what triggers religiously significant experiences in an individual? Memories of church and tradition—sitting in a sanctuary, singing certain songs, hearing stories of Jesus, engaging in certain prayer practices—are a well-recognized set of triggers. A second set of triggers are multiple life situations—"situations of sickness and vitality, of questing for truth and struggling for justice, of loving and reconciling, of pondering the vastness of space and of traveling the inner, endless journey of the psyche, people come upon the reality of God."

Shea observes that the second set, life situations, seems to be the more traveled path to religious awareness today. The presence that people used to find in the dark back of Gothic churches they now claim they find in the bright light of the secular world.[48] A special sanctuary with high-quality finishes and maybe stained-glass windows was a trigger for spiritual awareness for countless generations. But such a setting, like the back of Gothic churches, does not work so well for younger generations—the post-moderns—who work out their faith through engagement with the world around them. They are attracted to "EPIC" worship—experiential, participative, image-driven, and communal, in the acronym proposed by Leonard Sweet.[49] This can happen easily in a gym.

What triggers religious experiences depends a lot on the upbringing of the adult. Ever since the collapse of the Sunday-school movement several decades ago, most young adults now have a set of triggers different from their parents.

Understanding the Meaning of the Experience

John Shea uses a quote from T. S. Eliot: "We had the experience but missed the meaning." Men and women of today undergo events that, with the eyes of faith, are authored by the Spirit. But the religious significance of these events often goes unheralded. While the Spirit is the permeating energy of the experience, his work is not recognized. When the experience is seen in purely secular terms, then its God-power does not break into consciousness.[50]

It is important that the telling of the experience be in story form. If we give only the pattern of experience, we cut short the process of personal appropriation of the experience through the story. Storytelling has a power of involvement and appreciation that the mere noting of patterns or the talking about experiences analytically does not have.[51]

Here are some more nuggets:

- ✓ Psychology and sociology can *illuminate* what happened, but in the last analysis, they cannot *determine* what happened. It becomes explicitly religious when the one with the experience judges it to be a time of contact with a transcendent otherness. Divine reality has made itself felt.[52]

- ✓ The divine is not nakedly apprehended but intuited by what it is making happen.[53]

- ✓ In the excesses and pretensions of the Spirit, we look to the Memory of Jesus for direction and perspective. But when Memory threatens to alienate us from the depth of the present, we look to the Spirit to bring us life. Spirit and Memory are critical correctives.[54]

- ✓ When we retain the message of the King but lose the feel for his presence, the passion of religious mission turns to dull obligation.[55]

- ✓ Religious traditions die because they lose touch with their God. Religions usually degenerate in the end into a rationalistic theology, a formal morality, or a ritualistic cult. Sometimes a religion that is nothing more has ceased to live.[56]

- ✓ Within the Christian tradition, many have deplored this process of development and adaptation. For them, every change has smacked of betrayal. Others have welcomed development. For them, change is a sign of vitality.[57]

CONVERSION OR AWAKENING?

Telling your story, according to John Shea, is very important. Stories have to have words. Which words are best?

Conversion stories are favored and well told in believer-baptizing churches in America, in contrast to infant-baptizing churches. Some, indeed, are of radical change from one way of life to a new life in Christ. How God does this can be fascinating. But many similar stories can be told by those who grew up in a Christian community and at least passively confessed the faith. Then something happens, and their faith takes on new meaning with energetic Christian living. Is that a conversion? Here is the place to explain why "awakening" is a better word for most major faith stories.

Conversion

Conversion is inadequate for three reasons. First, it does not cover people who have known from the beginning of memory that they are children of the triune God. To imply they were not Christians until this special, later experience denies the foundational understanding of God's grace applied by infant-baptizing churches.

Second, "conversion" does not set up the born-again for subsequent peak religious experiences on their journey toward Christlikeness.

The life transformation called conversion is an attractive research topic for psychologists of religion. The *classic* paradigm is sudden conversion, like that of Paul's initial encounter with Christ. But there is a new *emerging* paradigm for research that recognizes gradual conversion. It has these characteristics: conversion occurs gradually; it is more rational than emotional; it is a process of self-realization; it is not permanent and may occur several times. No one experience is representative of all conversions.[58]

Third, conversion is an inadequate translation for the word used in Scriptures. Those who talk about conversion experiences usually cite the Greek *metanoia*, which means, literally, "change of mind." Yet in all but one instance, the NIV translates this word as "repentance." To repent means to be sorry, to regret past ways.

Is it better in ministry to focus on conversions or on repentance? Repentance is much the bigger concept and broader approach that applies to all who are seeking Christ. Where you are coming from is not as important as where you are now and where you are going. God cannot do much with someone who is full of himself or herself. His Spirit can accomplish more with those who are sorry for their past sins and faulty allegiances.

Awakening

There has to be a better word than conversion to describe this lifelong process of transformational steps on the way to becoming more like Christ. Let that word be "awakening." It is biblical. Paul tells the Romans to wake up from their slumber and to clothe themselves with the Lord Jesus Christ (Romans 5:11). He tells the Thessalonians not to be like others who are asleep but be alert and self-controlled, putting on faith, love and hope (1 Thessalonians 5:6–8). Is not this a call to awaken to more fruit of the Spirit?

There is a coherent theology behind this emphasis on awakening. The eighteenth-century continental Pietists chose awakening as their key word for the renewal of life in Christ, so much in need by nominal Christians and their churches at that time. They emphasized biological instead of traditional legal language and put a heavy emphasis on growth as God's work to make things new. Resurrection power was a key concept. The God who is good enough to justify persons is also powerful enough to change their lives. (This Pietist approach is further explained in my essay "A Coherent Theology for the Work of the Spirit Today," which you can find at the end of this book.)

The apostle John ends his gospel by telling us that Jesus did many other things beyond those he just reported. John observes, "If every one of them were written down, I suppose that even the whole world would not have room for the books that would be written." If those in that generation would fill a whole book, what would the book look like twenty centuries later, with eighty generations of billions of Christians telling their story of encounters with Jesus through his Word. Almost all of those are lost in history.

But we who are alive now can carry on the noble tradition by telling our stories, by witnessing personally to present generations. Join the parade. Tell your faith stories.

PART IV
How to Shape a More Spirit-Oriented Church Culture

CHAPTER 7
Modify Your Church Culture to Thrive Spiritually

> The wind blows wherever it pleases. You hear its sound,
> but you cannot tell where it comes from or where it
> is going. So it is with everyone born of the Spirit
> —JOHN 3: 8

> For you did not receive a spirit that makes you
> a slave again to fear, but you received the Spirit
> of sonship (by which we are) brought into the
> glorious freedom of the children of God.
> —ROMANS 8:14, 21

On a recent fall Saturday, several people from church and I were pulling weeds in the yard of an elderly widow—we had never met her, and she was not from our church. Two others were cleaning her basement. We were among 350 from church who went out on Servant Saturday morning to do just that—serve others in the community with no ulterior motive. Just finding enough work for that many was a major organizing project, done by a staff member. She worked through the city government, whose staff identified mostly elderly in need of help. The mayor showed up after our breakfast to send us on the way. He seemed genuinely moved. It was a win/win for everybody involved.

What brought my church, Royal Redeemer Lutheran near Cleveland, to that Saturday morning? It was an outgrowth of staff discussions about new ways to accomplish our goal: to make and grow disciples. Our new logo features three words: Connect, Belong, Thrive. We want to *connect* with many in our suburban community, purposely *include* them in our church community, and help all participants *thrive* in their spiritual life. The third—thrive—is the hardest.

This new effort aims to develop a church culture that includes generous service to others. We know generosity has to be a consistent theme in sermons. We highlight the joy that comes from being generous to others. We know this behavior has to be modeled by staff. We know servant behavior is more likely to happen when opportunities are organized to do this with others. We are learning how to help participants thrive in just this one aspect of spiritual growth.

"Thrive" is indeed the new frontier for mission-minded congregations. Helping church participants not just grow but really thrive in their personal spiritual life is the challenge for churches wanting to do better in their ministry in the future.

Twenty-five years ago saw a movement among conservative Protestant churches called Church Growth. The emphasis was on numeric growth of participants in a congregation by learning from churches that *had* grown, some to tens of thousands of attendees on a weekend. One observation was that congregations needed to make a conscious decision to grow and then remove barriers. In effect, they changed their church culture to more openness to the unchurched. Seeker services became popular, aimed beyond the members to visitors. This intent to *connect* with others brought significant changes to the church culture of many congregations.

Parallel was the small group movement of the 1980s and '90s. In the suburban environment, it is hard for one person to relate with a sense *belonging* to hundreds of others that he or she does not know. Thus, many church leaders today strive to foster small-group interaction for Bible study and mutual encouragement. This effort makes a lot of sense, but in our experience, it is hard to accomplish and sustain. Yet the result is so important that we keep plugging away at making small groups a part of our church culture.

There is growing evidence that the movement today is toward *thriving* in the Spirit. In chapter 3, I featured how the Spirit-oriented Pentecostal movement keeps growing worldwide, while the strongly Word-oriented traditional church bodies are in decline. One study of a thousand Protestant congregations identified the sixteen "most vibrant, spiritually alive congregations" of which they were aware. By my assessment of their websites, three-fifths of those are highly Spirit-oriented. Yet Pentecostal congregations make up only one-fifth of the Protestant churches in America.[59]

Another large-scale research effort identified "passionate spirituality" as one of the most important characteristics of healthy, growing congregations.[60] In discussions I have had with leaders in traditional church bodies, someone will inevitably observe that "passionate" and their tradition is an oxymoron—a contradiction. This is a sure formula for decline.

Think about it! What unchurched person would want to become part of a congregation where participation does not seem to make a difference in the lives of those involved, at least from their outsider perspective? To state the case differently, why would someone want to participate in a congregation where most do not appear to be thriving spiritually?

DECIDE TO THRIVE SPIRITUALLY

One of the observations from the Church Growth movement was that in order to grow numerically, a congregation has to decide consciously to grow and then remove barriers that stand in the way. The same can be said for congregations that want to thrive spiritually. This happens best with a conscious decision to cultivate soil for the Holy Spirit and to remove church-culture barriers that block the Holy Spirit from doing his renewing work among those gathered as the congregation. One thing is certain: greater spiritually is not going to happen by doing the same old things the same old ways among the same people.

I *am not* advocating imitation of Pentecostals. Basic spiritual temperaments have to be respected. Protestants from northern European cultures (home of Lutherans, Calvinists, and Anglicans) seem to have inherent resistance to strong emotional displays. I once observed a two-hour Pentecostal service in which the pastor, knowing I was there, pulled out all the stops for emotional displays. Feeling emotionally abused, I was eager to leave when the end finally came.

I *am* advocating that congregations get back to basic spirituality. Jesus wants us to worship in spirit and truth. The truth part is largely under human control through what is preached and taught. But truth without spirit is barren. Objective truth needs to become subjective, and that is the Spirit's work. Paul wants us to become Christlike, and this certainly involves righteous behavior. But the specifics of the behavior are not as important as the heart condition for doing them. Changing hearts should be the objective, and this is the Spirit's work.

Paul understood the human heart as the workplace for the Spirit sent by God. He tells the Romans that it is with their hearts that they believe and are justified (Romans 10:10), and that God poured out his love into their hearts by the Holy Spirit (Romans 5:5), who knows our hearts better than we do (Romans 8:27). He tells the Ephesians he wishes the Father's love may strengthen them with power through the Spirit in their inner being, so that

Christ may dwell in their hearts through faith (Ephesians 3:17). Softening hearts is the Spirit's specialty.

Since the Holy Spirit is involved, the results are unpredictable. He moves as he pleases. What works for some does not bring the same result for others. It is much easier to deal with heads and teach for knowledge. The time-honored, village-church assumption is that head knowledge turns into heart conviction. For many, this did happen—but too often in a superficial way.

In today's urban areas, however, Christian beliefs and values are under constant assault. Deeper conviction comes through experiences of struggle. Churches can welcome such struggle among participants as the workplace for the Spirit. They can learn how to adapt their support to individual circumstances. But first needs to come a commitment to follow the Spirit's unpredictable ways.

There is much talk about spirituality in our American culture these days. Definitions vary widely and can include almost anything beyond material existence. But recognize this: if you are talking spirituality but are not focused on the Holy Spirit, then you are not talking biblical Christian spirituality. Part of consciously developing a church culture for thriving in the Spirit is to get back to Bible basics.

THE HOLY SPIRIT AND CHURCH ORGANIZATION

I had invited seminary staff from my area for a barbeque on the deck of our home. Unlike many other men, I don't enjoy this ritual. Soon after I put the chicken pieces on the grill, a flame burst out and got bigger from the fat drippings on the hot coals. I figured I could control that by lowering the hood and reducing the size of the air vents. It worked. The flame went away. But when I looked again ten minutes later, there was not only no flame but also no heat. I can't remember what we did for the chicken part of the meal, which obviously did not go as planned. But that evening I recognized and have not forgotten this event as a metaphor for dealing with the Spirit in a church.

A flame is one of the two classic symbols for the Holy Spirit who came upon the apostles at Pentecost. The other is sound like the blowing of a violent wind. Jesus himself blessed wind as a metaphor for the Spirit at work. He explained to Nicodemus, "The wind blows wherever it pleases. You hear its sound but you cannot tell where it comes from or where it is going. So it is with everyone born of the Spirit." The analogy works better in the original Greek, where the word for wind, *pneuma*, is the same as for spirit. We have it today in English when we talk about *pneumatic* tools that are driven by air pressure, like the hand tool used to take wheels of a car in a tire shop. The Spirit is that pneumatic power in Christian lives.

The problem comes when Jesus explained that you cannot tell where the wind is coming from or where it is going. Such wind is unpredictable. So is the Holy Spirit. We humans have limited tolerance for the unpredictable. We like to have reliable control over what will happen in the future.

Rather than risk a burst of damaging flame in church life, we prefer to limit the amount of oxygen of the Holy Spirit getting into what we are doing together as a fellowship. Experienced grillers would have known how better to handle my crude attempt to control the chicken barbeque. Experienced church leaders can learn how to better control the Spirit's work without putting out his flame.

Max Lucado offers a helpful image for how to welcome the Spirit into our lives and fellowship. Living in Texas, he appreciates the cool air in his writing room. He cannot take credit for the compressor. It came with the mortgage. But he also has to open the vents in the room. "I did not install the 'air makers,' but I did open the 'air blockers.' Cool air fills the house because the vents are open."[61]

Change the reference point to Ohio and to a furnace rather than an air compressor. The analogy gets even better. Do you want more of the warmth of the Spirit? Open up the "air blockers"—the vents.

FACE LEADERSHIP FEARS

Look for the oxygen of the Holy Spirit in the motivations of individual believers. Expect participants to contribute to the common good what the Spirit moves them to do in their different, unique ways. But is not this a prescription for chaos as participants get in each other's way, heading in different directions? Certainly, this can happen—in the absence of wise leadership. Thus, Paul emphasized the second part of the Spirit's movement; that is, to grow within each the fellowship-building fruit of love, patience, trust, kindness, gentleness, and self-control—all of which are basic to working together peacefully. So, yes. Spirit-inflamed believers can bring stress into a church community. But with cultivation of a congregation's soil, the Spirit also can work out the solution through character changes that bring unity. The result can be a very exciting church community that furthers the kingdom of God in the lives of those they touch.

Protestant congregations today should recognize two kinds of fears that can drive their decision making. One is having so much spiritual energy that the fellowship bursts apart from all the activity. The other is having so little spiritual energy that their church fades away. The first is hardly a realistic fear for the many withering congregations today. They would do better to run the risk of letting in more of the Spirit and his special energy.

Fresh energy usually happens when the Spirit brings into the fellowship those believers who are new and have a different perspective. In my church plant, three families from Pentecostal/charismatic backgrounds were active for several years and then moved on. Meanwhile, they modeled for us an exciting prayer life that still characterizes the congregation.

In so many ways, the apostle Paul was personally fearless in his mission work. He recognized that "you did not receive a spirit that makes you a slave again to fear, but you received the Spirit of sonship [by which we are] brought into the glorious freedom of the children of God" (Romans 8:14, 21). Congregations can learn to reduce slavery to fear with the freedom inherent in Paul's understanding of their life together.

A major step toward more freedom in church life is to become more tolerant of differences in the spiritual journey of participants and to loosen expectations of the one best way. This means reducing dependence on traditions as the guide to what will be done in the future and being open to new approaches. To do so means resisting the urge to solve problems by making more rules. Take it from a specialist in organizational behavior: tighter organization is not necessarily better organizing when it reduces flexibility to adapt to changes happening in the organizations environment.

Traditional congregations that want to foster the work of the Spirit in their midst will need to consider changes in their church culture. This is especially true for those that carry on the old culture of village churches. What a church culture consists of and how to change it will be described more carefully in Chapter 8.

For now, see the challenge as changing a church's traditions. Anyone with experience in Christian congregations knows how strong resistance to change can be. Lurking behind such resistance is usually fear—fear of the unknown, fear of loss, especially loss of control. Paul would ask then if such a congregation has become a slave to fear. He would remind us that the Holy Spirit wants to bring believers into the glorious freedom God's people can enjoy (Romans 8: 14, 21).

LOOSENING UP A TRADITIONAL CHURCH ORGANIZATION

Consider some options for how we organize our *relationships* and our patterns of *communication* together. Both are matters of church culture. A culture is an integrated pattern of knowledge, beliefs, and behaviors that determines what is learned and transmitted to future generations. The emphasis here is on behaviors. The same beliefs can shape different behaviors. In chapter 8, I will explore how a culture of behavior usually trumps beliefs. To change a culture, you have to change behaviors.

Patterns of Relationships

One time-tested way to reduce conflict in a village is to separate the leader from the rest; that is, to recognize clergy as distinct from the laity. The really important religious activities are reserved for only the clergy to do, who are distinct by years of schooling and who come from outside the village. The role for the rest is to support by praying and paying for the real ministry.

The apostle Paul would have had a hard time understanding this way of organizing. He would certainly agree that spiritual leaders are important, but he would expect believers to emerge in these roles through proven ability that would affirm a special calling by the Spirit. From the village perspective, Paul's understanding of everyone being gifted by the Spirit for a specific function in the body would make no sense. No wonder his emphasis disappeared for centuries.

In my church plant, one of the leaders was well respected for his wisdom. I learned much from him about how to disciple others. One of the other leaders complained that Norm just wanted to be pastor. My reaction was, God bless him. How can I help?

Patterns of Communicating

Part of organizing a congregation can be seen in patterns of communication. In a village, it is almost all one-way communication, from the pastor to the people, who are assumed to have little of value to share. Their responses are fully scripted and their songs carefully selected from hymns composed in the past. If worship is to be in spirit and truth, the safer approach is to emphasize carefully controlled truth, even at the expense of spirit.

I am advocating widespread stories telling of personal encounters with the Spirit. This approach stands in contrast to the pattern of traditional churches. The old assumption is that laypeople have little of spiritual value to offer. They are to receive insights, not give. But encouraging them to share how the Holy Spirit influenced their lives can open our eyes to how the Spirit works. Such sharing can prepare us for how, in God's grace, we too can grow under the influence of the Spirit. It is important that their stories be told in ways appropriate to the situation. Sensing when and where a constructive time is calls for reliance on the fruit of wisdom that the Spirit can provide.

The leadership challenge is to organize more ways in which such sharing can happen. Some churches do provide time in public worship for testimonials. There is little precedent in mainline churches, and participants usually do not have experience for telling their stories well. One way to introduce faith stories is to have them videotaped and then edited into a more compact form. But then someone has to spend time on the project. This can be an opportunity for the leaders to pray that the Father send his Holy Spirit to motivate someone to step forward for this specialized video ministry.

We have to assume that constantly evolving communication technology is part of God's ongoing creation. The intent to use more of new communication technologies can in itself provide more opportunity for the Spirit to touch lives. Learning how to use such technology can become one more challenge for church leaders who want to turn around decline.

OFFERING NEW CHURCH EXPERIENCES THE SPIRIT CAN USE

A new word has emerged to describe some religious experiences that are beyond most mainline Protestant traditions. These are "threshold" experiences. If you like a fancier word, anthropologists speak of "liminality." A threshold is a sill at the bottom of a doorway into a different room. These experiences view a familiar truth or relationship from the fresh perspective of standing in a different room.

Short-term mission trips to work in a very different culture of another country are great threshold experiences for many participants. A lot of congregations today do one-week trips in support of ongoing work of a Christian church or community in a less-developed country. "Life-changing" is often the reaction to observing the poverty and the faith of these fellow Christians. Their stories can also help change their congregation, as they bring back new enthusiasm for mission that stimulates others to look for ways to reach out. My mission interest has as much to do with church renewal at home as it has with impacting lives of others to whom we are in mission.

Weekend renewal events can be another threshold experience for those involved. Precedent is set by programs variously called Cursillo, Walk to Emmaus, Via de Cristo, or Faith Alive, in different denominations. Those programs are now in decline because of difficulties recruiting participants to spend three or four days away from home, spouse, and family. "Celebrate Journeys in Christ" is a version we are working on. It shortens the format to a Friday evening and all day Saturday. This happens at the church, so that participants can go home for the night. Key to the experience is having leaders give a short personal testimony, a faith-witness about what God has done in changing their lives. These stories become the basis for small-group discussions. The discussions help stimulate in participants a reflection on what God has done in their lives. Their stories, in effect, become a personal witness by testimony, which gives hope and encouragement to others, many of whom had no idea what was happening spiritually in the lives of fellow church members they have known for years. We ask participants to plot out on a graph paper the line that would reflect the ups and downs of their spiritual life over the years—their personal spiritual journey. Then we invite each to share in his or her small group what those low points and high points were. Most are eager to tell their discoveries.

Both kinds of threshold experience give expression to what Paul called the many-faceted wisdom of God (Ephesians 3:10). A facet is a face or surface. Diamonds are cut to have many facets that reflect light in different directions, giving the "bling" to a diamond ring—the more facets the more bling. Preachers have long practiced proclaiming different perspectives on Christ's life and work, like seeing him as shepherd, bread of life, vine, or living water. These many facets are held up for view by those sitting in the pews. Another way to change perspectives is to move people out of the pews into very different settings, like someone's living room, or a mission trip, or a renewal weekend.

Christian church cultures have changed dramatically over the centuries as churches, under the Spirit's influence, adapted to new countries and changing circumstances. Those that did not change became mostly footnotes in church history. Those who want to insist on maintaining their traditions today might want to ask which tradition they choose, because over the centuries, long-established church bodies have changed some of their dominant traditions with every generation. Change can be good. This is what the Holy Spirit specializes in.

BE OPEN TO SUPERNATURAL INTERVENTIONS

One of the stories we tell at church concerns a ten-year-old girl who was shopping with her mom on a Saturday evening. Her speech became garbled. Fearing the worst, Mom took her to the hospital emergency room. Danielle had had a brain aneurism. Physicians told the mother to prepare for the worst. If the girl survived, she would not talk or walk. We prayed for her in the Sunday services. At about 11:00 a.m., a large group gathered to pray some more. That afternoon, the nurse reported that the girl woke up about 11:00 a.m. and talked and walked. She has turned into a beautiful young woman who regularly attends our services with her mother. Thank God for answered prayer.

Was this a miracle? Or was it just an unusual coincidence, perhaps based on a misdiagnosis?

The central issue of this book is whether God interacts with people in supernatural ways today. Traditional mainline churches confess that the third person of the Trinity is active in general, but for all practical purposes, they have no expectations of the Spirit's supernatural work in lives and churches today. I have kept the focus on observable changes in the inner motivations and feelings of believers. What about changes visible in the bodily condition of a person—changes for which there is no natural explanation? In other words, does God do healing miracles today?

Part of my spiritual journey has been to gain confidence that indeed the supernatural God of the Bible can and does intervene in otherwise unexplainable ways now, as he did in biblical times. This journey took me to Nigeria as part of a medical team in the crusade of Uma Ukpai— Miracle Worker. I did what I call Prayer for Healing services, at which a leg lengthening happened. I am impressed with a colleague in our very traditional, "miracles-ceased" Lutheran church body who was very ill, went to one of Benny Hinn's "Miracle Crusades,"and was restored to full health. Now he and his wife have their own healing ministry. At a retreat, I heard a hospital pathologist, who reads the initial biopsy and the one just before surgery, remark that indeed cancers do disappear "more often than you think." Much of what I learned about prayer for healing came from a retired, otherwise traditional Presbyterian pastor from Canton, Ohio, Rev. Donald Bartow.

In my own research, through a random survey of 366 Lutheran pastors, I found that 75 percent had experienced or witnessed a miracle, defined as an event for which there is no natural explanation. Yet in our church culture, we never talk about this.

The issue was settled in my mind years ago. Doubts about the supernatural Spirit's involvement in natural affairs, like doubts about the special inspiration of Scriptures, have largely gone away. I attribute this to the Holy Spirit's work on me. It certainly makes possible much greater appreciation of the apostle Paul's robust theology of the Spirit at work in churches today—a theology that gives powerful purpose for the work of Christian congregations.

Actually coming to the conclusion that God can indeed be supernaturally involved in human affairs should logically lead into a whole change in worldview, something that is indeed now happening in Western culture. Let seminary professor Luther Halverson explain what happened to him personally when he recognized the results of intercessory prayer for others.

> This cultural revolution suggest a shift in one's mode of being and doing that so radically reverses, upsets, and disorients that it amounts to a conversion or a passage through Alice's mirror. In it the same reality is seen, the same data observed, but everything is different, perhaps even opposite.
>
> Although the empirical and experiential are part of the data reviewed with new eyes, I believe that the change has more to do with vision than analysis, serendipity than calculation, the Holy Spirit than prescribed ritual and dogma.[62]

It is easy to disprove a negative. All you have to do is find one exception. The negative at hand is that God does not intervene in supernatural ways. After years of inquiry, my conclusion is that this negative proposition is false. Evidence keeps mounting that God does intervene supernaturally. I am confident that Danielle's healing was a miracle.

DEVELOP A SPIRITUAL COUNTERCULTURE IN YOUR CHURCH

The kind of Spirit-oriented church culture that I envision would be counter to three other cultures that Protestants encounter today: (1) the classic Reformation teaching that miracles ceased in the New Testament, (2) the emotion-laden Pentecostal crusades seen on television, (3) university culture with a one-dimensional view of reality.

1) Counter to "No More Miracles"

The Reformation happened against the backdrop of widespread medieval superstition and belief in miraculous power of shrines and relics. Against such beliefs, the very rational John Calvin taught, "Those miraculous powers and manifest workings, which were dispensed by the laying on of hands, have ceased; and they have rightly lasted only for a time."[63] We are to look for the miraculous in the everyday creative ways that God provides for our health and well-being. Thus supernatural interventions ceased after Christianity was established in the first century.

Luther was somewhat more open-minded but not much. He prayed for his colleague Philip Melanchthon, who was at the brink of death, so that Melanchthon later wrote how he was recalled from death to life by divine power. Luther laid out an order of service based on James 5 for a pastor to use to help an individual named John Korner. But little came of this. The result was the very same cessation assumptions in the Lutheran church doctrine and history that I experienced. The bottom line for traditional churches of the Reformation was, don't expect supernatural interventions in any practical way today.[64]

The most difficult position to maintain, it seems to me, is this cessationist view that God could intervene now like he did in Bible times, but he chooses not to do so today. There is certainly no biblical evidence for this perspective. It is not a logically coherent position. It has the consequence of depriving many Word-oriented churches of the increased spiritual power that comes from greater openness to the working of the Holy Spirit.

2) Counter to "Do Special Things to Get God Moving"

Vineyard Pastor Ken Blue provided valuable perspective for my journey of understanding miraculous interventions. He joins many other mature Pentecostals in warning against what can be called a "faith formula." This is a view that if you just know enough, repent enough, and pray enough, you will get special blessings and gifts of the Spirit, including healing. He notes that this view largely accounts for the volume of noise and emotionalism at some healing meetings—a frenzy they think will get God moving.[65]

This intent to get God moving on our schedule by our actions can be a form of work righteousness for salvation, where getting right with God depends on what I do, not on his initiative. But the function of biblical faith is not to get specified results. It is to trust God in his love to take the initiative to give what is good for us. This is grace in action. This grace needs to stay central in a church culture fashioned for our times.

I have worked out for myself that miracles do happen but are rare, perhaps 1 percent of the time. Some observers estimate 2–4 percent. But even 1 percent is enough to demonstrate the possibility. Might 1 percent be enough to change a worldview in general and ministry practices in particular? To me, it is enough to warrant changing a church's culture to more openness to the Spirit's movement among those gathered.

3) Counter to One-Dimensional University Culture

What kind of reception can you expect if you share a miracle experience? You will probably be heard with interest. Sociologist Robert Wuthnow, in his study of spirituality in America, reports recent national poll results that find 83 percent of Americans agree that miracles are performed, even today, by the power of God. Another study reported that 68 percent of Americans definitely or probably believe in miracles. Even among people who seldom or never attend religious services, a majority think miracles probably happen. Where you will find pushback is among people with graduate degrees, only 18 percent of which definitely believe in miracles.[66]

University culture is distinct. But this is changing, according to Craig S. Keener, Ph.D. from Duke University. In his 2011 two-volume publication *Miracles*, he reviews the credibility of miracles from all possible viewpoints, summarizing issues and citing cases.

Keener notes how philosophers of science acknowledge that even fundamental principles—presuppositions taken for granted—must be open to revision in the light of further discovery. Such paradigm shifts become revolutions in worldview, in ways of conceptualizing the universe. Theories succeed by proving more persuasive than their competitors, but once they become dominant, they are displaced only with difficulty. Keener points out that academic politics can play a role in their resilience. Thus, some resistance to new extra-normal claims from around the world is not surprising, "though the quantity of these claims is now becoming overwhelming." He goes on to observe,

> [Academic] consensus does not determine truth, and many statements of consensus are premature in any case. Some older modern theologians like Bultmann declared that "mature" modern people do not believe in miracles, and that "no one can or does seriously maintain" the NT worldview. Those following such an approach can examine miracle account's theological and social functions while dismissing their historical foundations. Yet even as some theologians were demythologizing the Bible to make it relevant for an anti-supernaturalist audience, belief in miracles was rising among the Western public.[67]

POST-MODERN OPPORTUNITIES

The irony is that in contrast to older modernist pacesetters, younger generations have become post-modern. The term is vague but in general describes a movement in reaction to the assumed certainty of scientific efforts to explain reality. Post-moderns are typically not ready to accept the institutional church and its teachings, developed over centuries. But they are open to a reality beyond what can be proven empirically. Miracles and supernatural power are not dismissed out of hand.

Paul Prather summarizes,

> We Westerners, particularly, are becoming more open about the possibility of divine intervention today because the Enlightenment paradigm on which we so long depended has failed us miserably ... At the same time certain breakthroughs in the theoretical sciences such as physics have suggested that our cosmos is not the closed, precise, predictable universe that Newtonian scientists assumed, but rather that it contains quirky, unpredictable agents and events.[68]

A growing dissatisfaction with a one-dimensional view that recognizes only the material world can be seen most clearly in former Communist countries, like China. There, Christianity is growing rapidly. Most of that growth is occurring in churches that have high expectations of the Holy Spirit.

For someone of my generation, with a graduate university background, this openness among the educated to supernatural interventions is a big deal. It calls for a two-dimensional view of the world that sets aside old certainties and offers new opportunities for daily living. For churches, readiness to recognize that the Holy Spirit can indeed empower ministry and improve relationships should have major implications for how ministry is done.

To put this most dramatically, if there is credible evidence of one true miracle—a special event for which there is no natural explanation—that should be enough, logically, to demolish an old one-dimensional worldview.

The culture of a congregation usually does change from generation to generation, even if only a little. Influences come from many directions. Open up your congregation to ideas and emphases of more Spirit-oriented congregations, starting with those closest to your tradition. Be willing to listen to insights and values of the young generation of post-moderns. Your future may well depend on new ways of appreciating the Holy Spirit's work today.

CHAPTER 8

Change the Behavior to Change the Culture

You will receive power when the Holy Spirit comes on
you; and you will be my witnesses in Jerusalem, and in
all Judea and Samaria, and to the ends of the earth.

ACTS 1: 8

The last several decades have seen new forms of competition force a sorting
out in traditional ways of doing business, running schools, and staffing
the military. Cheaper goods from abroad put price pressures on American
manufacturers, leading to downsizing, sending jobs offshore, and adopting
more responsive organization structures. The Internet is reducing sales in
retail establishments and driving newspaper and magazines out of existence.
Widespread dissatisfaction with educational attainments of grade schools
and high schools is forcing a new performance-based school culture. With
no draft and ongoing wars, military forces had to adopt new ways to attract
recruits and retain veterans. The new army has been forced to change its
old ways.

In short, most businesses and organizations in American society have
faced increased competition and the need to change their culture for how
things are done. Just about anyone over age twenty-five can describe changes
they have seen and how they personally have adapted.

Churches face the same social forces today: more competition and
higher expectations. More competition comes not only in the form
of neighboring bigger churches with more program offerings, more
sophisticated communication, and better facilities but also in the presence of
many more alternative ways to spend Sunday morning, like youth sporting
events. Higher expectations turn into loss of loyalty and greater readiness
to go someplace else when "this church doesn't meet my needs." Mainline
Protestant churches in America had grown used to depending on loyalty
to sustain membership and ministries. There is much less tolerance now for
poor performance, especially with worship and sermons that fall short of
engaging the participants.

Many churches are apparently resigning themselves to the inevitable
withering that comes with loss of younger generations. Some pastors hope
the end is far enough in the future to see them through to retirement.

A better response to this higher bar for congregations that want to
remain healthy and effective is to become less reliant on tradition and more

intentional about what they are trying to accomplish. Usually, moving in that direction necessitates changing a congregation's inherited church culture.

A "hard" environment, by the way, is not uniform across American society. The "soft" environment will hold longer for churches in rural areas and small towns, where social relationships are more stable and participants are more willing to adjust their expectations. In those circumstances, decline will be from greater migration of youth to the big cities for more opportunities.

It is suburbia where the performance level needs to be increased because of more competition. Mobility is greater and fewer church participants know each other from encounters beyond the congregation. Shared memory is decreasing. The harder environment means that the status quo of many congregations will not hold long.

RECOGNIZING A CHURCH CULTURE

Anyone who has done church shopping knows the feeling of entering a worship service and feeling energized. It may be hard to figure out why, but the culture comes across as attractive. The opposite is to enter a service and feel the energy draining away. The reason why may be hard to identify, too. But as in so much of life, first impressions mean a lot.

Many church leaders and members would claim that such judgments are unfair because these observers do not appreciate the depth of what has been offered. They should learn first and then decide. That may have worked in previous generations, when so many felt obligated to be part of a church— or, to say it differently, they felt guilty if they were not. But that sense of obligation is increasingly hard to find in twenty-first–century America. If people are looking for a church home, they want something positive out of the experience, right from the beginning.

One small example would be a congregation's attitude towards "C and E Christians," who come only on Christmas and Easter. The faithful tend to look down on such "visitors," and their attitude expresses itself in aloofness and stray comments. A mission-minded church, on the other hand, appreciates these two opportunities to deliver a worship experience that will draw them back. Laying on guilt, as many historic churches do, may be counterproductive for drawing someone closer to Christ in that congregation. Church cultures of the future will focus on offering opportunities for personal benefit.

The dictionary definition of a culture is an integrated pattern of *knowledge, beliefs,* and *behaviors* that determines what is learned and transmitted to future generations. Most congregations today can tell you what they know and believe, but few are aware of how their behaviors form a distinctive church culture. For trying to figure out why their ways are not transferring well to their young, the first place to look is at the behaviors their culture models. Often, a younger generation sees what is or is not being done, of which the elders are not even aware.

You can describe a church culture with answers to questions like these:

- ✓ When someone not from the congregation observes a Sunday service, what mood would he or she pick up?
- ✓ When someone inquires, "Tell me about your church," what stories are told?
- ✓ How many young families and children are participating?
- ✓ What do participants expect to happen during the worship?
- ✓ Who shares leadership of the church with the pastor?
- ✓ Who gets recognized and affirmed and for what achievements?
- ✓ Does the church have clear direction for the future, and how widely is this affirmed among members?
- ✓ What is the level of creativity and enthusiasm among the participants?
- ✓ What does the condition of the physical facility tell about the values of members and leaders?
- ✓ How are decisions made, deferred, or delayed?
- ✓ Does the church talk mostly about the past or the future?

These are just a few lead questions to focus attention on who the people are, how they interact and behave, and what they value the most. All this is in contrast to what is said or written about their intentions and motivations.

One summer, I was chaplain at a county juvenile detention center. I thought we would get our Sunday worship off to a good start by singing the rousing "A Mighty Fortress Is Our God." I still remember the pianist's puzzled look. It took only a few measures for me to figure out this Lutheran standard was not known in this group. Time to switch to "Holy, Holy, Holy," which was played and sung with gusto. I was that naïve about how church cultures differ. That naïve, many Christian leaders are today about the limitations of the church culture they are used to.

Christian Schwarz is a contemporary German theologian and church researcher. He offers a framework for recognizing and describing key church dimensions in his Natural Church Development Survey. It consists of ninety-one statements that assess how often a participant does or observes specific behaviors. The result is an assessment of an individual congregation's church culture. The eight qualities or characteristics are leadership, ministry, spirituality, structures, worship service, small groups, evangelism, and relationships.[69]

Schwarz makes no pretense of being objective about what these qualities should look like in a healthy, effective Christian congregation. He presents an adjective in front of each quality:

empowering leadership	gift-oriented ministry
passionate spirituality	inspiring worship service
functional structures	holistic small groups
need-oriented evangelism	loving relationships

Any congregation today can use this questionnaire to understand better the strengths and weaknesses of their specific church culture. It is available through Church Smart Resources at www.churchsmart.com.

What makes this questionnaire special is that it focuses on observable behaviors rather than on beliefs or values. In our increasingly unchurched national culture, our behaviors become the primary witness to those not yet drawn to Christ. Our behaviors in turn reflect how Christlike we live. Jesus knew that the ability for such living comes only by the power of the Spirit. So he told his disciples that to be witnesses to the end of the earth, they first need the Spirit to fall upon them (Acts 1: 8). In fact, they should wait for this power from on high (Luke 24: 29) before they go to all nations.

Without lives changed and empowered by the Holy Spirit, our witness as Christians today in an increasingly hostile environment will likely have little impact. We need to move beyond words to behavior—to behaviors that communicate God's love not just for us but others we encounter.

A FEW PRINCIPLES ABOUT ORGANIZATIONAL CULTURE CHANGE

The reason to change a church's culture is so that the congregation can do its ministries more effectively in the future. Leading a culture change is challenging work.

In business, the culture of a corporation is a huge topic for management. Sophisticated systems are used to analyze the culture present in any business or organization. The intent is to bring changes to that culture in order to increase productivity or some other outcome necessary for the organization's continued success. Usually, increased competition calls the future into doubt and provides the incentive to make changes.

For churches, too, increased competition and decline provide the main incentive to understand and change church cultures. In the 1950s, all Christian churches and their cultures were doing well in terms of planting new churches and growing in membership and attendance. This is not so anymore for mainline churches and increasingly for many Evangelical churches. Recognizing that the future is in doubt for many congregations can give incentive to assess the culture they inherited and to consider change.

Here are some principles from corporate culture change that are applicable to churches:

1. Changing an organization's culture is anxiety-provoking. Edgar H. Schein authored the most popular textbook on organization culture and leadership used currently in business schools. He explains that the culture "provides its members with a basic sense of identity and defines the values that provide self-esteem. Cultures tell their members who they are, how to behave toward each other and how to feel good about themselves. Recognizing these critical functions makes us aware why 'changing' culture is so anxiety provoking."[70]

If these basic functions are true in a business, think how much more they apply to a church, which is all about providing basic identity and values and moral basis for behavior. No wonder change is difficult for churches. Approach the remodeling of a church culture with caution.

2. A second principle is that strong leadership is needed to change an organizational culture. Without strong leadership to challenge current ways, congregations will settle back into what is familiar and comfortable. The key leader, of course, is the pastor. Effective change has to involve other leaders, but it is the pastor who decides what to feature and functionally has veto power over how much emphasis will be placed on other initiatives. Pastors typically have their core expertise in the ways of the old culture. Few are prepared to negotiate changes to something with which they themselves have little experience. Many do not even consider themselves leaders to begin with. A question in any church is whether the pastor is up to the challenge. The job is less difficult if other leaders are ready to understand and support.

3. Culture change inevitably brings conflict between those who like the old and those espousing the new. By personality, most pastors are inclined

to avoid conflict, if possible. To lead change necessitates skills in handling conflict as part of managing changes in a church.

4. Leaders have to earn the right to be followed in new behaviors. In Schein's words, "Whatever is proposed will only be perceived as what the leader wants. Until the group has taken some joint action and together observed the outcome, there is not as yet a shared basis for determining whether what the leader wants will turn out to be valid."[71] Some sort of success for new ways is crucial, even in a church.

5. Culture arises through shared experiences of success. It makes sense to earn credibility by starting with relatively small changes that are easy to do and are welcomed by almost all. Negotiating these easy changes will build trust.

6. Culture trumps vision. So declares Samuel Chand. Vision is about *ideas*. Culture is *behavior*. Culture change is all about turning new ideas into new action that past behaviors would resist.[72]

In short, until words turn into successful actions, not much will change in a church culture. Preaching a new emphasis is a good start. But until it results in action, persistence on that theme can turn into nagging that annoys more than motivates. In most cases, who needs to initiate the action? It is the pastor or leader who wants the change. Putting words into action usually takes organizational skills in arranging opportunities to express the desired behaviors.

Sometimes a growth spurt in a congregation is preceded by an "igniter" event. This is an event, often not planned, that allowed the congregation to experience success, which brought about new energy and openness to change. I am aware of one congregation that took on a service project of cleaning up the city park nearby. A TV crew came to interview them and produced a segment on the evening news. With this visible success, the leaders were then ready to put more energy into exploring new ideas for ministry.

WHERE TO START CHANGING A CHURCH CULTURE

A culture has three components. If a church's culture is no longer functioning well, is the problem that their culture has insufficient *knowledge*? Or are their *beliefs* poorly expressed? Or are they perhaps emphasizing the wrong kind of *behavior*?

Knowledge

The easiest part of a church culture to deal with is the knowledge base. Maybe they don't know they are dying or that God is still alive and active throughout the world. It is easy to gather data to show where a congregation is failing and to describe what it should be doing. Denominational officials sometimes try this approach, proclaiming with alarm, in the case of my church body, that a huge proportion of congregations have not added more than one new member in the previous several years. What does this accomplish? Not much, beyond making these many congregations feel guilty, unappreciated, and even angry. In general, guilt seldom produces innovative new ways of meeting a challenge.

A ministry colleague tried to set a new direction by bringing in guest speakers to show how congregations in general can become self-centered and dysfunctional. Long-time members inferred that the pastor did not appreciate them and rebelled against his contemporary worship efforts. He had to leave. Additional knowledge itself seldom is a vehicle of change. More important is to get the knowledge hooked up to beliefs and behaviors of a specific congregation of people. The hooking together is the leadership challenge. Culture change does not happen in general. It takes place when behaviors are changed step by step.

Beliefs and Values

Then how about changing a church's beliefs? Protestant churches are typically all about beliefs—at least the type that get expressed as doctrine. To understand all those differing doctrinal emphases requires going back into church history to understand issues that arose among Christians, usually in a given country in a specific century. Try to explain the beliefs that distinguish Southern, Northern, or General Baptists without explaining a lot of their histories, like the Civil War. Most pastors are highly concerned about teachings and work hard to explain their truthfulness. Most members are less interested in the specifics; their values are much more pragmatic.

When I did my doctoral dissertation on pastors as organizational leaders, I visited and interviewed fifty-six suburban pastors of mainline denominations. One overall impression gained from looking at bulletin boards and publicity is that they all showed similar church cultures of events, groups, and social activities. The names differed, but the expectations were about the same. Although Presbyterians, Lutherans, Episcopalians, Methodists, and United Church of Christ have different belief emphases, they were all doing roughly the same things.

Consider this as evidence that distinctive church beliefs really do not drive Protestant churches' culture. Any new behaviors need to be consistent with the beliefs. But beliefs are usually not the place to start the cultural change process. Work first on behaviors that express the beliefs.

All churches say they value mission to others. They recognize and accept the Great Commission to take the gospel to others. But somehow, many never get around to doing much about it. Their own immediate congregational needs take priority, especially if they are financially challenged. How dollars are spent is a fairly good measure of value placed. Another good measure is time spent. Does anybody go out of the way to serve someone else beyond the congregation? Probably some do so individually, on their own. But is it a shared church value?

The way to find out is for a leader to propose some specific mission-minded behaviors that do not cost anything but time. The minister could preach ten sermons on the Great Commission, but the values of a church's culture will not change until some new behaviors emerge. This will happen best if doable, specific opportunities are organized and made accessible. To change a church culture, start with specific behaviors, and then deal with the differing values.

Basic Underlying Assumptions

Organizational culture specialist Edgar Schein makes a helpful distinction between espoused beliefs and values and then the barely expressed basic assumptions underlying an organizational culture. Most difficulties in remodeling a culture come not from dealing with stated beliefs but from running into unstated underlying assumptions. These basic assumptions are difficult to confront, tend to be non-debatable, and hence are extremely difficult to change.[73] Such assumptions are called "theories in use" in the field. Congregations often have theories in use that have little relation to the espoused theology.

Thousands are the stories of pastors who come to a congregation with the intent to take it in a new direction, only to discover stiff, debilitating resistance in a year or so, to the dissatisfaction of all. The desired change is usually in the direction of turning around decline through worship and program changes intended to be more appealing to the unchurched. Often, the pastor has the assurance of the call committee that the new direction is exactly what they want. The basic underlying, unexpressed assumption for most members, however, is that their church culture should stay the way it is. Of course they want the pastor to bring new members, but usually taken for granted is that the new ones should be like the present ones, enjoying and doing what they themselves enjoy and do.

Behaviors

The positive behaviors to aim for in changing a church's culture have been discussed in previous chapters. The goal is to modify a congregation's culture to be more open and inviting to the Holy Spirit's movement in their midst. To that end, congregations are encouraged to do more of the following behaviors: Ask the Father to send the Spirit in specific ways. In appropriate circumstances, tell stories of how the Spirit worked recently. Celebrate progress in personal spiritual journeys, especially in the form of major awakenings to a higher level of spiritual understanding. Offer a greater variety of opportunities for religious experiences. Be willing to recognize God's supernatural interventions in healings and to pray for them.

INFLUENCES ON BEHAVIOR IN CONGREGATIONS

What are the options that church leaders have for ways to change behaviors in a congregation and thus its culture? Right out of the MBA class lectures on Social Psychology of Work Organizations that I taught, I offer four sources of influence on the behavior of those doing cooperative effort:

1. *Formal messages* are mostly expectations put into writing, such as job descriptions, goal and policy statements, or messages of encouragement.

In churches, look for policy statements, by-laws, and of course sermons. Unlike other organizations, churches have a pulpit with expectations for a formal message each week. Any anticipated change needs to have the reasons for it enunciated. Basic to good communication is to use words mostly familiar to the listener and therefore speak and write with lots of words from the church's tradition, adding just a few new words or concepts gradually. Remember, culture trumps vision.

2. *Informal group messages* that affect behavior are those of others in the work group who interpret that which they should pay attention to and thus, that which can be ignored. The filter is usually whether or not there will be any consequences for ignoring what the boss says.

Church people usually bring powerful filters with them, especially if they have heard hundreds of sermons. For those who come to church out of habit, the first challenge is to get and hold attention. The filter is whether the message applies to them personally. In the church I serve, we are working on ending each sermon with next steps and then having these listed for check-off on a registration Connection Card, gathered after the message. The next steps usually involve some organized activity.

Two different kinds of church cultures can be distinguished on the basis of the informal conversation of participants after the service is over. In my tradition, this is mostly small talk that could be heard in almost any social setting. I admire those churches where participants actually talk about the message or worship and bring God into their conversations. Getting from the first to the second is a tall challenge.

3. *Technique messages* are delivered by the established work flow. Keeping up with the assembly line determines most of the behavior of factory workers. Office workers find themselves spending hours in front of a computer screen. As is so evident in recent decades, new technologies necessitate different behaviors.

"Technique" is a good word for church use. A worship service employs many different techniques, such as how prayer is done. Is it exclusively by the pastor reading written prayers, or delivered informally? Does the congregation join together, speaking written prayers, or are they encouraged to break into small groups for shared prayer about what is on their minds? Is the order of service taken from a hymnal, or from a folder customized for that weekend, or presented on an overhead screen? Is the singing done sitting down or standing up, led by an organ or a praise band, from the front or the back? These are just illustrations to raise awareness. A good exercise would be to note all the different techniques used in a worship service and then think back on alternatives that could be tried instead.

Church cultures are traditions developed as customs, and customs are made up of accepted techniques. The easiest way to start changing a culture is to try specific new techniques. The easiest techniques to change are those usually regarded as the pastor's prerogative, such as standing behind a pulpit or by the first pew, or leading prayers differently. But at some point, small changes add up to new customs that raise anxiety about whether the old ways were inadequate, and members feel devalued. Then the leader is dealing with basic assumptions that are barely recognized. That is when the skills for managing church conflict are put to the test.

4. *Action messages* are what participants find themselves actually doing. Words have turned into action. If participants find themselves cleaning someone else's house on a Saturday morning, they are asking basic questions

and rediscovering values that their church stands for. Usually, such activity needs to be organized to provide an occasion.

In general, the influence of a message source on behavior goes from the most powerful at the bottom to the least powerful at the top of this list. Action messages are the most influential, while formal messages are the least. Most church cultures assume the top-down approach and too often never get to action messages. If you want to change a church culture, change what participants actually do; move beyond just preaching about it.

HOW NEHEMIAH CHANGED AN OLD TESTAMENT CULTURE OF GOD'S PEOPLE

The Old Testament book of Nehemiah offers a great illustration of how to change a church culture. The year was about 448 BC. Nehemiah, from the community of Jewish exiles in Babylon, was a court administrator for King Artaxerxes. He felt called to take a leave of absence to return home to help his kinsmen rebuild the Jerusalem walls that were destroyed in 587 BC, when Judah rebelled against Babylon. On site, after assessing the situation for three days, Nehemiah called together the Jerusalem leaders, focusing attention on the obvious security problem of having no walls. Then he announced his plan. The next day, all Jewish men found themselves hauling stones and beams and witnessing progress, restoring the wall. For most, action came before understanding the full rationale.

It was crucial that Nehemiah organize assignments according to family or neighborhood groupings—so important that the names and assignments are all preserved in Nehemiah 3. There was lots of social pressure to conform to the plan. Nehemiah knew how to work through natural group leaders and let them fill in the specifics in their own way.

After the wall was built (in only fifty-two days), Ezra, their spiritual leader, gathered everybody before the water gate and read the Word of God (the Torah) all morning, and the Levites then explained it. On the twenty-eighth day, Ezra led them all in a time of repentance, followed by a covenant agreement that the leaders signed. Then the wall was dedicated. Ezra and Nehemiah made one of the greatest preacher/administrator teams of all times.

The sequence was action messages, supported by group messages, and finalized with dramatic formal messages.

HOPE FOR A REMNANT

Many Christian churches in America today face the kind of future the Israelites experienced before the return of Ezra and Nehemiah. Those chosen people of God were a discouraged remnant of what used to be a flourishing and exciting community. Today, the effects of the accelerating forty-year decline of traditional Protestant church bodies are making evident that a very large proportion of congregations are well along in the withering process—mostly gray hair with few young families and shrinking numbers as the elderly pass on.

That Israelite remnant must have thought God had abandoned them. Of course, he had not. God had many plans for his people. But his ways took new forms when he sent his Son to call forth a new people of God that became Christianity. Then he called the apostle Paul to new experiences of the timeless Holy Spirit and to explain to Christ's followers how the Spirit works in their lives.

Withering Christian congregations need to ask what kind of problem they are facing. Do they have a God problem that he has abandoned them? Or is the problem that their particular traditional church culture no longer fits well with the emerging changes in American culture?

The fact is that God's Christian church is alive and flourishing in other parts of the world. The Holy Spirit is changing an ever increasing number of people around the world. Just as the Israelites at Nehemiah's time could not anticipate what God did in the New Testament 450 years later, so American Protestants, just one hundred years ago, could not have anticipated the rise of highly Spirit-oriented Christians here and around the world.

Here is the choice: Protestant congregations can insist on staying with all of the traditions and forms they know from previous generations. Or they can watch how the Spirit is moving today and open themselves, step by step, to such movement in their midst. Is a congregation's cultural heritage definitive for all times, or can it be a solid foundation for remodeling work to stay better in step with the Spirit and times?

A good leader will help the congregation make an informed choice about how they will face the future. Some fresh movement of the Holy Spirit will have to happen to even step up to such choice, let alone make it.

Accept the challenge to cultivate the soil of church life and to open up the vents for the Spirit's pneumatic power. Take the challenge of sailing close to the Spirit wind. Ask the Father to send his Holy Spirit to guide the process. Then see what happens. You might be surprised!

Your Encounters with the Holy Spirit: Name and Share Them—Seek More

Permission is given to make copies for discussion purposes.

Discussion Guide for
CHAPTER 1
What Has the Holy Spirit Done in Your Life Lately?

If fathers know how to give good gifts to their
children, how much more will your heavenly Father
give the Holy Spirit to those who ask him!

—LUKE 11:13

1. What is your personal response to the following question?

"What has the Holy Spirit done in your life lately? The Spirit
brought me into saving faith. True. But what about lately, say, in
the last month or two?".

2. How well does the following statement describe your view?

"Too often we gain the impression that the Spirit was some kind of
vague ghostly presence only in Bible times."

3. Would you consider the rhythm of name an encounter with the Spirit,
share it with others, and seek more an improvement in Christian living?

4. How can Jesus' famous promise of a response to asking, seeking, and knocking make more sense when applied to sending the Holy Spirit?

"My answer is that he wants us to ask for specific movements of the Spirit among specific people. He wants us to form clear expectations so that we can observe when in fact the Spirit has moved. We are more likely to see what we expect than to notice something we are not looking for."

"Christians can be trained to see what many other Christians miss." (page 4)

5. What is supernatural motivation? Would you agree with the following?

"Appealing to the more basic human needs (bodily, security, affiliation, status) did indeed enable the Spirit to energize Christian churches over the centuries. But human motivation alone has its limits, especially as our American culture becomes increasingly unchurched. It is time to learn how to appeal to the supernatural motivation offered by the Holy Spirit."

"In terms of human motivation this can be called 'self-actualization.'"

6. What is the difference between emotions and feelings in church life? Does the following make sense to you?

"Here is the issue: Do the emotions come first before you rationally figure them out? Such "raw" emotions are too often not of the Spirit and can become destructive. Or do feelings flow from reasonable perceptions based on Scriptures? Such feelings can be the bedrock of church life."

7. About the psychology behind name, share, and seek more:

   a. What is likely to happen to an encounter if it is not named?

       What do you think of these names—Spirit encounter, spiritual experience, a God moment, a Holy Spirit sighting, an awakening? Which name would you use?

   b. What is likely to happen if a life-changing encounter is not shared? Why is it important to share this with others who are Christians?

   c. Why is it important to seek more such encounters? What does the Father promise?

       You are more likely to see something if you are _____.

       How do you seek more encounters with the Spirit? (To be discussed further in chapter 5.)

Discussion Guide to
CHAPTER 2
How Do People Experience God in Their Lives?

The Holy Spirit touches human spirit.

JOHN 3: 6

The Advocate, the Holy Spirit, whom the Father
will send in my name, will teach you all things and
will remind you of everything I have said to you.

—JOHN 14: 26

1. Is there a more basic question for Christians and their leaders to ask in this twenty-first century than, "How do people experience God in their lives today?" Would you agree that

"Ways previous generations experienced God are not working as well now in younger generations. When and how do believers attach trust and feelings to the gospel? Faith without feelings remains superficial and probably boring."

2. Can your recognize a difference between the rational language of heads and the feeling language of hearts?

We can learn from the Bible about the many promises God makes to his people. The details are worked out in doctrine books. These address head knowledge. To find out how God's people feel about his actions and promises, we need to turn to language different from logical propositional truths. Feelings are expressed best in images and metaphors of poetry.

3. What are your favorite feeling images from Psalm 23, "The Lord Is My Shepherd." How do these various images make you feel?

> The Lord is my shepherd, I shall not want. He makes me lie down in green pastures, he leads me beside quiet waters, he restores my soul. He guides me in paths of righteousness for his name's sake. Even though I walk through the valley of the shadow of death, I will fear no evil, for your rod and your staff, they comfort me. You prepare a table before me in the presence of my enemies. You anoint my head with oil; my cup overflows. Surely goodness and love will follow me all the days of my life, and I will dwell in the house of the Lord forever.

4. Hallmarks of "religious experience" are feelings of peace, presence of God, and empowerment. Can you recall a special time when you had any of these as an experience of God?

5. Have you personally experienced any of the following, which are ways Paul recognized the Spirit at work (see text for passages)?
- ✓ greater understanding of faith
- ✓ less temptation
- ✓ less enslavement to fears
- ✓ desire to do more ministry in church
- ✓ more willingness to sacrifice something
- ✓ a special feel of unity with other Christians
- ✓ a greater sense of love, joy, peace, patience, and gentleness

6. Have you witnessed the Spirit at work in others in the following ways, which Paul recognized as the Spirit's influence (see text)?
- ✓ someone encountering Christ's call and deciding to follow
- ✓ presentations of the Word that bring greater insight

- ✓ someone's new life in Christ becoming more evident
- ✓ someone coming to church through a personal invitation
- ✓ better relationships when two or three come together in Christ
- ✓ a Christian showing special boldness or wisdom in witnessing
- ✓ Christians singing with special gusto and intensity
- ✓ someone experiencing freshness and renewal in his or her faith

7. Can you envision the Holy Spirit as a dove sitting on your shoulder and whispering into your ear something God would have you do?

Can you recall a time when you heard such a whisper and acted on it?

8. How can you tell when it is the Spirit whispering?

What do you think of Jonathan Edwards's distinction between unreliable and reliable signs of the Spirit?

Reliable Signs:
- ✓ a lasting indwelling that brings an evident new nature
- ✓ a new spiritual sense that does not come from self-interest
- ✓ new kind of conviction and humility
- ✓ hunger for God
- ✓ Christian practice

9. What is your reaction to the following statements about getting more of the Spirit?

"You can't get to the grace for Christian living and service on your own. Lasting growth in love, peace, patience, and other godly fruit has to come as a gift of God through his Holy Spirit. So how do you get more of these gifts? In short, you ask for the Spirit to work on you to change your heart, and then you put yourself where the Spirit can do his work."

Discussion Guide to
CHAPTER 3
Seek the Gifts and Fruit of the Spirit

Now about spiritual gifts, brothers, I
do not want you to be ignorant.

—1 CORINTHIANS 12:1

The fruit of the Spirit is love, joy, peace,
patience, kindness, goodness, faithfulness,
gentleness and self-control.

—GALATIANS 5:22

1. What has been your experience with Paul's teaching on spiritual gifts in 1 Corinthians 12?

2. Have you witnessed special energy for ministry?

"Paul's major point in 1 Corinthians 12 is that in each congregation of believers, the Spirit is already at work, motivating all participants to contribute different acts of ministry for the common good. This is motivation very different from reluctantly serving on a committee."

3. What would make Paul's teaching on *charismata*—gifts of the Spirit—controversial today?

4. What has been your experience with Paul's teaching on fruit of the Spirit, as explained?

"He distinguishes a subset of spiritual gifts that he calls the greater gifts for the most excellent way of living together as a congregation. Chief is love, without which fulfilling life together is difficult. To the Galatians, he describes these as fruit of the Spirit."

5. What are the fruit of the Spirit?

What words would you use to describe what the fruit of the Spirit are that Paul lists in Galatians 5:22—love, joy, peace, patience, kindness, goodness, faithfulness, gentleness, and self-control?

Are they emotions? Feelings? Characteristics? Something else?

6. How are the fruit of the Spirit related to fellowship, as explained here?

In his benediction at the end of his first letter to the Corinthians, Paul chooses "fellowship" as the key characteristic of the Holy Spirit. "May the grace of the Lord Jesus Christ and the love of God and the *fellowship* of the Holy Spirit be with you all."

7. Do you think the switch to turn the lights up for the Spirit is set at low or at high in traditional churches of the Reformation?

"In effect, the Reformers set the dimmer dial of the light switch on low for the third person of the Trinity."

"Historically we keep the dimmer switch dialed low for heart change. The challenge for low-expectation churches is to dial up the dimmer switch to expose more of the work of the Spirit in changing hearts."

9. What do you know about Pentecostal churches and the charismatic movement of the1960s and '70s? Are you aware of the following?

"By any standard, the growth of Pentecostal expressions of Christianity has been phenomenal. A hundred years after its start in 1906, the movement worldwide was estimated to include 558,000,000 adherents."

Discussion Guide to
CHAPTER 4
The Spirit Brings Growth beyond Conformity

And we who reflect the Lord's glory are being
transformed into his likeness with ever-increasing
glory, which comes from the Lord, who is the Spirit.

—2 CORINTHIANS 3:18

You are God's garden. I planted the seed,
Apollos watered it, but God made it grow.

—1 CORINTHIANS 3:6, 9

Do not conform any longer to the pattern of this world,
but be transformed by the renewing of your mind.

—ROMANS 12: 1

1. Do you or does anyone in your group have experience with life in a village
or small town? What is your impression of the emphasis on conformity in
village life?

2. When the proportion of a population goes from 85 percent rural and small
town to 85 percent urban, what can you expect to occur in the traditions of
a congregation in the new setting? Said differently, what can you expect to
no longer happen in urban church life as it used to occur in villages?

3. How important do you think freshness and change are in a church?

"In contrast to such conformity, the apostle Paul recognized that the hallmark of the Holy Spirit at work is freshness and change."

4. Do you agree with the following?

"Many congregations and pastors wind up doing the same old things with the same people in the same old ways and thereby close the door on what new things the Spirit might want to do among them. The Spirit's inclination is to change people, not leave them in a rut."

5. Can you recognize these as remnants of village-style ministry?
   a. Fourteen-year-old confirmation of children baptized as infants
   b. Emphasis on separation between clergy and laity

   Are there any other remnants of village-church culture you can recognize?

6. What would you guess to be the definition of Christian maturity in a village church?

Compare that to Paul's definition:

"Paul's understanding of maturity is quite different. No one ever reaches it. He tells the Ephesians that their local body of Christ should continue to be built up until all become mature, reaching to the height of Christ's full stature (Ephesians 4:13). Because the standard is Christlikeness, we will never reach full maturity as a Christian in this life." (See 2 Corinthians 3:17, 18; 2 Thessalonians 1:3; Colossians 1:6; 2 Corinthians 9:10.)

7. What is your reaction to the claim that for Paul, life in Christ and life in the Spirit are one and the same thing?

"They are two ways of describing the same experience. To become more Christlike is to be filled more by the Holy Spirit." (See note 27 at end of the book for parallel passages.)

8. Gardener, Builder, and Shepherd

Paul "saw himself as a gardener and a builder—perspectives that got lost over the centuries in favor of the shepherd image, which Paul himself does not use."

What comes to mind with the traditional image of the pastor as a shepherd?

What would you expect of a pastor as a gardener?

What comes to mind as a spiritual temple that a pastor might try to build up in a congregation?

9. Do you think that individuals have different spiritual temperaments?

What do you think of the nine different pathways highlighted by Gary Thomas: Naturalist, Sensate, Traditionalist, Ascetic, Activist, Caregiver, Enthusiast, Contemplative, Intellectual?

Discussion Guide to
CHAPTER 5
Cultivate the Soil of Personal and Church Life

Repent . . . and you will receive the gift of the Holy Spirit.
—ACTS 2: 38

1. What is your first reaction to using the metaphor of cultivating the soil of personal and church life to prepare for the Spirit's fresh movement?

2. How useful for you are the following three images for approaching God in repentance?

    a.   The Pharisee and publican (Luke 18).

    b.   God resists the proud but gives grace to the humble (James 4:6).

    c.   Isaiah's "Woe is me. I am ruined" (Isaiah 6:5).

3. What would you look for to see a hard path, rocks, or weeds in your personal spiritual life?

4. What do you think would happen if a pastor viewed the congregation as the topsoil for pastoral work?

5. Does your congregation have hard surfaces? If so, how would you break them up?

6. Does the soil of your congregation have a lot of rocks? If so, how would you deal with them?

7. How can you add more soil to your congregation, even without adding new members?

8. Does your congregation have weeds in its soil? What would you look for? How would you deal with them?

9. Can you imagine calling your whole congregation to a day of repentance? Of what should it repent? How would you envision that happening on such a Sunday?

Discussion Guide to
CHAPTER 6
Share Stories of Personal Spiritual Journeys

Since we live by the Spirit, let us
keep in step with the Spirit.
—GALATIANS 5:25

1. Can you recall a car of yours whose odometer (count of miles traveled) brings back happy memories? Why?

2. Share a little bit of your personal spiritual journey in Christ. When did it start? What were high points? Would you care to share any low points?

3. Luke uses the unique and helpful phrase, "full of the Holy Spirit," which he then couples with a specific characteristic to describe what that fullness brought—joy, wisdom, faith, witnessing boldly.

Can you recall a time when you were unusually "full of the Spirit"?

4. React to the following interpretation of Paul:

"He wanted primarily that believers be filled by the Holy Spirit, to the point of having so much of the Spirit that his gifts and fruit overflow in their lives of abundance."

5. Where would you place yourself in the following four stages: Exploring Christ, Growing in Christ, Close to Christ, and Christ-Centered?

6. Another description envisions a productive Christian "hitting the Wall"— an obstacle they cannot overcome with their ordinary efforts and skills.

Have you ever "hit the wall," or do you know someone who has?

7. How important is struggle in a Christian's spiritual journey? Would you agree with the following?

"Struggle cannot be taught. It happens one by one through personal response to unique circumstances. But we can observe what it is like in others and learn how God worked it out their lives. It is the personal struggle of a 'before' condition that sets up the compelling 'after' story of a movement to greater convictional faith."

8. How helpful do you find the distinction between a stage 3 faith ("I believe what my church believes") and a stage 4 faith of heartfelt conviction?

9. John Shea writes about "triggers" for personal experiences of religious significance. These can be surroundings, like a Gothic cathedral, or life situations, like serious illness. In your personal life, what have been triggers for your special encounters with the Holy Spirit?

10. Have you ever had a truly transforming experience that changed your life? Do you know anyone who has?

What words have you used or heard to describe such a personal transformation?

11. Do you or your church have a good balance between Spirit and Memory? Would you agree with John Shea?

"When a church lives just on Memories it loses touch with God. An excess of Spirit, however, needs to be corrected with Memory of what has happened in such circumstances in the past."

12. What is your reaction to focusing on awakenings rather than on conversions?

Discussion Guide to
CHAPTER 7
Modify Your Church Culture to Thrive Spiritually

The wind blows wherever it pleases. You hear its sound,
but you cannot tell where it comes from or where it
is going. So it is with everyone born of the Spirit

—JOHN 3: 8

For you did not receive a spirit that makes you
a slave again to fear, but you received the Spirit
of sonship (by which we are) brought into the
glorious freedom of the children of God.

—ROMANS 8:14, 21

1. Is "passionate spirituality" characteristic of your congregation? Would
you agree with the following?

"In discussions I have had with leaders in traditional church
bodies, someone will inevitably observe that 'passionate' and their
tradition are an oxymoron—a contradiction. This is a sure formula
for decline."

2. How can a congregation purposely decide to thrive spiritually?

3. What meanings have you heard applied to the word "spirituality"? Would you accept the following?

"If you are talking spirituality but are not focused on the Holy Spirit, then you are not talking biblical Christian spirituality."

4. Jesus explained that like the wind, the Spirit is not predictable. What is your reaction to something important that is not predictable?

5. Which is the greater danger for your church? Would you agree with the following?

"Two kinds of fears can drive their decision making in a church. One is having so much spiritual energy that the fellowship bursts apart from all the activity. The other is having so little spiritual energy that their church fades away."

6. Do you have experience with a short-term mission trip or a weekend renewal event?

How can they become a spiritual experience?

7. Have you experienced or do you know someone who experienced a miracle, defined as an event for which there is not natural explanation?

8. Does your church heritage teach that miracles ceased after the New Testament? What is your reaction?

9. What is your reaction to special healing services you may have seen on TV?

10. Have you ever struggled with modern university culture that assumes a one-dimensional view of the world—all that exists is what can be observed and measured?

11. What do you know about the movement called "post-modernism"? How does it present an opportunity for Christian witness?

Discussion Guide to
CHAPTER 8
Change the Behavior to Change the Culture

You will receive power when the Holy Spirit comes on
you; and you will be my witnesses in Jerusalem, and in
all Judea and Samaria, and to the ends of the earth.

—ACTS 1: 8

1. American institutions are undergoing rapid change because they now face more competition and higher expectations. Do you think this is true for churches too?

2. Corporate cultures have been purposely and steadily changing in recent decades. Have you experienced culture change at work or in schools?

3. What do you recognize in the culture of your congregation that could be changed without changing basic beliefs?

4. Why is changing an organization's culture anxiety-provoking?

5. In what ways is success necessary for a good pastor? Would you agree with the following?

> "Leaders have to earn the right to be followed in new behaviors. Some sort of success for new ways is crucial, even in a church."

6. How does "culture trump vision"?

> "Vision is about *ideas*. Culture is *behavior*. Culture change is all about turning new ideas into new action that past behaviors would resist."

7. Do you think congregations resist change because they do not have enough knowledge of what is happening around them?

8. What are some of the unstated assumptions that would make culture change difficult in your church? Use this definition:

> "A helpful distinction is between espoused beliefs and values and then the barely expressed basic assumptions underlying an organizational culture."

9. How helpful is the distinction between formal messages, like sermons and job description, and the action message that participants find themselves doing?

10. What do you think are the most influential messages to send when trying to change a corporate or church culture?

11. What are the most helpful things you have learned in these discussions of *Your Encounters with the Holy Spirit*?

KEY AND SUPPORTING PASSAGES ON THE WORK OF THE HOLY SPIRIT TODAY

CHAPTER 1

If fathers know how to give good gifts to their children, how much more will your heavenly Father give the Holy Spirit to those who ask. —Luke 11:13

Unless I go away, the Advocate will not come to you; but if I go, I will send him to your. John 16:7

The Spirit will take from what is mine and make it known to you. John 16:15

You have received the Spirit who is from God that we may understand what God has freely given us. Acts 1: 12

The Spirit himself testifies with our spirit that we are God's children. Romans 8:16

CHAPTER 2

The Holy Spirit shapes human spirit. —John 3:6

The Advocate, the Holy Spirit, whom the Father will send in my name, will teach you all things and will remind you of everything I have said to you. —John 14: 26

You know the Spirit, for he lives with you and will be in you. John 14: 17

Those who live according to the Spirit haves their minds set on what the Spirit desires. Romans 8: 5

You are controlled by the Spirit, if the Spirit of God lives in you. Romans 8: 9

I speak the truth in Christ—my conscience confirms it in the Holy Spirit. Romans 9: 1

God put his Spirit in our hearts. 2 Corinthians 1: 22

I pray that out of his glorious riches he may strengthen you with power through his Spirit in your inner being, so that Christ may dwell in your hearts through faith. Ephesians 3: 16

CHAPTER 3

Now about spiritual gifts, brothers, I do not want you to be ignorant. —1 Corinthians 12:1

The fruit of the Spirit is love, joy, peace, patience, kindness, good-ness, faithfulness, gentleness and self-control. —Galatians 5:22

The mind controlled by the Spirit is life and peace. Romans 8: 6

The Spirit helps us in our weakness. Romans 8: 26

CHAPTER 4

And we who reflect the Lord's glory are being transformed into his likeness with ever-increasing glory, which comes from the Lord, who is the Spirit. —2 Corinthians 3:18

You are God's garden. I planted the seed, Apollos watered it, but God made it grow. 1 Corinthians 3:6, 9

Do not conform any longer to the pattern of this world, but be transformed by the renewing of your mind. —Romans 12: 2

CHAPTER 5

Repent . . . and you will receive the gift of the Holy Spirit. —Acts 2: 38

Those who live by the Spirit have their minds set on what the Spirit desires. Romans 8: 5

If by the Spirit you put to death the misdeeds of the body, you will live. Romans 8: 13

CHAPTER 6

Since we live by the Spirit, let us keep in step with the Spirit. —Galatians 5:25

Through your prayers and help given by the Spirit of Jesus Christ, what has happened to me will turn out for my deliverance. (Paul's story) Philippians 1: 19

And in Christ you too are being built together to become a dwelling in which God lives by his Spirit. (Stories of congregations). Ephesians2: 21,22

CHAPTER 7

For you did not receive a spirit that makes you a slave again to fear, but you received the Spirit of sonship (by which we are) brought into the glorious freedom of the children of God. —Romans 8: 15, 21

We are ministers of a new covenant—not of the letter but of the Spirit; for the letter kills, but the Spirit gives life. 2 Corinthians 3:6

Now the Lord is the Spirit, and where the Spirit of the Lord is, there is freedom. 2 Corinthians 3: 17

Therefore, if anyone is in Christ, he is a new creation. 2 Corinthians 5: 17

CHAPTER 8

You will receive power when the Holy Spirit comes on you; and you will be my witnesses in Jerusalem, in and Judea and Samaria, and to the ends of the earth. —Acts 1: 8

Go and make disciples of all nations, baptizing them in the name of the Father and of the Son and of the Holy Spirit, and teaching them to obey everything I have commanded you. Matthew 28: 19

They were all filled with the Holy Spirit and spoke the word of God boldly. Acts 4: 31

Choose seven men from among you who are known to be full of the Spirit and wisdom. Acts 6: 3

They chose Stephen, a man full of faith and of the Holy Spirit. Acts 6: 5

ESSAY ON A COHERENT THEOLOGY FOR THE WORK OF THE SPIRIT TODAY

David S. Luecke

God is not only good enough to justify persons,
he is also powerful enough to change them.

This statement was the watchword for the Pietist movement in Germany and Scandinavia, roughly parallel in time to the Puritan movement in England. The grandfather of the movement was Johann Arndt, whose classic devotional book *True Christianity* was very popular for centuries among Protestants in and from those countries.

The thrust of the movement is captured in this statement by Arndt:

> True knowledge of Christ is ignited by the Holy Spirit in our hearts as a new light that becomes ever brighter and clearer like a mirror that is polished, or as a small child grows and matures daily in body. A man is newborn in his conversion if the righteousness of Christ is given to him through faith. Then the image of God will be daily renewed. He is not yet, however, a perfect man but a child who must yet be trained by the Holy Spirit and become conformed from day to day with Christ Jesus.[74]

The foremost scholar of Pietism in North America today, C. John Webord of the Evangelical Covenant Church, highlights these characteristics seen especially in writings of Arndt and Philipp J. Spener, the father of Pietism:

- ✓ a shift from legal to biological language
- ✓ a shift from external to an internal work of God
- ✓ a view that spiritual birth is as radically passive as physical birth; the chief actor is God
- ✓ heavy emphasis on growth—growth in knowledge but also growth in grace
- ✓ reliance on words like new-maker, resurrection power, re-generation, re-creation[75]

About 150 years after the Reformation, Spener, a high-level church administrator, addressed the condition of the state church under the influence of the "dead orthodoxy" of academic theology. About Spener, Weborg observes,

When the Pietists made the "new birth" the operative model for God's redeeming work, they derived from it the notion of renewal from the inside out. What starts small, develops. Applying this model to the church situation, P. J. Spener sought a way to renew the church from the inside out. In his thinking, one could begin in a small way with a few people and watch the "practice of theology" bear fruit.[76]

THE HOLY SPIRIT'S WORKPLACE

This late seventeenth-century Pietist movement provides the broader theological context for the understanding of the Holy Spirit's work that I present in this book. As Johann Arndt recognized, we need to be trained by the Spirit to become conformed from day to day into greater Christlikeness.

The leaders of this movement were pastors and church officials immersed in the practical affairs of congregations. They were reacting against generations of civil-service parsons (*Pfarrer*) whose interests often seemed far removed from practical care of souls in their parish. It is the Pietists who championed the title of "pastor" (Latin for shepherd) in order to lessen the emotional distance between the village parson and those in his care.

The Pietist agenda put them in direct conflict with the university-led proponents of orthodoxy (right teaching). While remaining orthodox in their Lutheran theology, the early Pietists wanted to balance that emphasis with focus on orthopraxis—right practice. They were contesting "dead orthodoxy."

In any conflict between advocates of clear thinking and those who feature hard-to-define feelings, the thinkers almost always prevail. In times of popular loyalty to church, clear thinking is good and supports a vibrant church life. In the twenty-first century, the defining issue is not so much dead orthodoxy as it is dead or dying congregations. This is a time to turn the focus back to the less precise world of feelings. The Holy Spirit is the key to understanding the "feelings" dimension of the body of Christ gathered at any specific time and place.

For most of Christian-church history, Paul's passages on the gifts and fruit of the Spirit were left on the periphery of understanding what is basic to the Christian life. I have argued that they really belong to the core of his approach to leading a congregation. Paul was a practical theologian. Most of what we know of his theology comes from his letters to specific congregations with particular real-life concerns. In recent centuries, theology became the domain of seminary and university thinkers, with a tendency toward ivory-tower idealism. Perhaps it is time to return the initiative to pastors who, like Paul, are rooted in congregational life.

THE SANCTIFIED LIFE

The proper doctrinal term for the topic in this book is "sanctification" that follows "justification." The Christian life—and thus, church life—is about both, and they can be easily confused.

Sanctification puts together two Latin words: *sanctus* (holy) and *facare* (to make), and thus means to make holy. *Just-ification* means to make just or right before God.

Three Aspects of Holiness

Let's stay with sanctification. The following is a definition offered by New Testament scholar Everett Harrison in the *International Standard Bible Encyclopedia*: "Holiness has a threefold aspect. 1) All believers are positionally holy by virtue of their calling as saints. 2) They are then summoned to such conduct as befits their new position in Christ. 3) They are to seek by God's help to grow and mature with the life of Christ as their pattern for appropriation."[77]

1. Believers are called holy.

To explain sanctification, we need to consider "justification." It simply means to be made just or righteous before God. How that is done is the first aspect of holiness—being positionally holy before God by virtue of being called holy by God. He does so by forgiving our unholy-making sins when we ask him to judge us by the merits won for us by his Son Jesus the Christ. He does so out of his grace, his unmerited favor. The apostle Paul teaches, "Because of his great love for us, God, who is rich in mercy, made us alive with Christ even when we were dead in transgressions—it is by grace you have been saved" (Ephesians 2:4).

Paul expresses a ton of theology when he salutes the letter recipients in Ephesus, Philippi, and Colosse as "all the *saints* in Christ Jesus." In his original Greek he calls them the "holy ones." Obviously, they are not holy in the sense of perfect. He usually is writing about some problem or another reflective of sins they are still dealing with. But God calls them holy, and so they are in his sight. This is positional holiness.

A major split among Protestants occurs with the understanding of how this happens. I write with the conviction that this is 100 percent a gift from God through the Holy Spirit's movement to work accepting faith in the heart of the one hearing the gospel. The alternative is to expect the hearer to make the commitment to believe the offer, perhaps at a time of special emotional conviction. The result may view saving grace as 95 percent God's work and 5 percent the recipient's work. In Reformed history, this is called Arminianism. In Lutheran history, it is synergism—working together. Through either the 100/0 or the 95/5 formula, God's grace is still effective for the salvation of all who call on Christ's name.

But one consequence of "working together" can be seen in later doubts and even despair on the part of Christians who are no longer sure of their salvation because they no longer feel as convicted as they did at their "conversion." They lose sight of the *fact* that God, through his Holy Spirit, initiated their belief, and they lose confidence that they have saving *faith*, which is effective regardless of how they *feel* about it on a certain day.

2. Believers are summoned to conduct befitting their new position in Christ.

When God calls us holy in his sight, he also summons us to aim for the Christlikeness for which he gives us credit in our justification.

Another consequence of the 95/5 formula is that it often leads to paying more attention to what *we do* than to what *God has done*. The life of sanctification can be confused with justification. This easily results in legalism that stresses external behaviors associated with sanctification, even without the more basic internal changed heart condition, daily brought by the Holy Spirit in the life of faith. Subtly, the effect of sanctification can seem to become the cause of justification.

Extreme legalism without the internal heart condition looks a lot like the Pharisees whom Jesus was continually scolding. Legalism can be very off-putting to those watching what it means to be a Christian, when they see just the very specific behavior demands without the changed hearts. When the Holy Spirit works in a Christian's life, the fruit is love, joy, peace, patience, gentleness, and kindness. Such lives are the effective witness to an unchurched secular society.

Another split among Protestants occurs around what happens at conversion. Do we leave sin behind and become a totally different, more God-pleasing person forever? If so, living holy is a realistic expectation for daily life, and the occurrence of sin is a disappointing surprise. Certainly those called holy by grace *should* show conduct befitting their new position in Christ. But the issue is how much emphasis to put on morally right behavior after the gospel has done its justifying work.

Too much emphasis placed on lawful, command-oriented living shifts attention away from the motivation of a heart changed by the grace-working Holy Spirit, reflecting more love, joy, and peace. It is a fact among believers that the remaining lifelong strength of sin is too great to count on complete and permanent behavior changes as evidence of the Spirit's work.

Conversion is not a one-time event. It needs to happen every day. Luther is realistic when he teaches that the old nature in us, the flesh, should, by daily contrition and repentance, be drowned and die with all sins, and again a new man daily come forth and arise, who shall live before God in righteousness and purity forever.

Victorian England was a time when proper behavior and Christianity were blended in popular understanding. Victorian aspirations became synonymous with being a Christian. At a time when people and buildings were covered with coal soot, they even claimed the Bible taught that cleanliness is next to godliness. In his 1951 now-classic assessment of *Christ in Culture*, H. Richard Niebuhr used Victorian England as an example of the Christ *of* culture, where Christianity is all about the behaviors of Christians.

Much of conservative Protestantism in America today has roots in Victorian English Christianity. The holiness movement in the United States in the latter part of the 1800s is closely related to the Wesleyan Methodism that became dominant in Victorian England.

An offshoot of that movement in America in the early 1900s was the Pentecostal movement, still going strong. These two wings of Methodism are often described as "perfectionist" and "charismatic." The perfectionist doctrine is most clear in the Nazarene statement of faith, that believers are to be "sanctified *wholly* subsequent to regeneration"; they must always behave in a perfect way. The Pentecostal movement was additionally shaped by the highly developed subjectivism of many Baptists.[78] With such understandings, sinful behavior in Christians often comes as a surprise.

Many American Christians expect Christian behaviors and values to be supported by civic laws of government. This posture would not have been understood by the Christians of the first three centuries, living as they did in a morally lax Roman Empire. They preferred to be known by how they loved each other and by the witness of their martyrdom.

Their understanding of the sanctified life of followers of Christ was that it applied to each personally. It was not behavior to be imposed on others who did not yet claim to know Christ. The apostle Paul made this distinction clear to the Corinthians: "I have written you in my letter not to associate with sexually immoral people—not at all meaning the people of this world who are immoral. What business is it of mine to judge those outside the church" (1 Corinthians 5:9, 12).

3. Believers are to seek by God's help to grow and mature with the life of Christ as their pattern for appropriation.

This third aspect of holiness is the one that is the most promising today for shaping a church culture that best expresses what God does with his people. It is the one that leads to featuring the perspective of the Pietists from around the 1700s.

Here is a repeat of Johann Arndt's teaching quoted in the introduction: "True knowledge of Christ is ignited by the Holy Spirit in our hearts as a new light that becomes *ever brighter and clearer* like a mirror that is polished, or as a small child *grows and matures* daily in body."

This is the perspective that leads to a new focus on spiritual journeys—on the way but not yet there. It underlies the encouragement for church leaders to reclaim Paul's self-image of gardener to guide their work today. Paul thought of himself as a gardener and a builder. Gardening comes first, so that there are Spirit-touched lives drawn into a spiritual partnership, pleasing to God. Building relationships is important because the Word that changes lives is often conveyed best through others as they share their experiences.

CHANGED HEARTS AND SPECIFIC BEHAVIORS

The spiritually necessary relation between changed hearts and specific behaviors is difficult to maintain over time. This is especially true for raising up a new generation in the church. Hearts changed by the Holy Spirit happen one by one. Until that occurs personally, the second-generation children and other observers all too readily perceive church life as all about the behaviors, which to them do not seem appealing. In truth, congregations are always only one generation from dying out when the heart-changing Holy Spirit is squeezed out of a church's life.

Pietists from around 1700 understood well the proper relationship. But that movement too, over time, lost the centrality of grace and focused too much on human effort. Piety took on the connotation of "holier than thou." The term "pious" came into use from the Latin title *Pia Desideria* that Philip J. Spener used for his book, advocating six proposals for reforming church life gone stagnant. A more accurate translation would be *Heartfelt Desire for God-Pleasing Reform*. The proposals included greater exposure to all Scriptures, more emphasis on how knowledge of faith should result in practice (orthodoxy accompanied by orthopraxis), that ministers should themselves be true Christians, and that sermons should be prepared so the outcome of faith and its fruits be achieved in hearers to the greatest degree possible. Since all ministers in the state church were university educated and often had a different perspective on their civil-service job, many looked with scorn on these Pietist ideas.

Today, piety is popularly regarded with the sort of disdain given to English Puritans, as killjoys with puritanically negative views on basic joys of life, like sex and drink. They are represented by the Church Lady on *Saturday Night Live*. Ironically, both the Pietists and the Puritans really did understand and experience high levels of joy that flowed from the truly spiritual source.

The modern term for piety is "spiritual formation." Thank God, this still has positive connotations. For some, spiritual formation means only trying to find a more meaningful way of life beyond material concerns. For many, this is spiritual life in general. But for Christians, it really is about spirit, as in the Holy Spirit.

Augustine of the fifth century, arguably the greatest Christian theologian, was certainly right with his observation, "Our hearts are restless until they rest in Thee." Truly distinctive Christian spiritual life is all about cultivating the soil of our hearts for the Holy Spirit's work to turn us toward God. Rightfully, the emphasis is on internal conditions, rather than the behaviors that result. The constant problem in churches is that the practices of spiritual disciplines get turned around so that the Christian life too easily becomes regarded as the cause of God's favor, rather than just the preparatory condition for the Spirit's ongoing works of applying grace in daily living.

PIETISTS IN THE NEW COUNTRY

My church body—the Lutheran Church–Missouri Synod—is a product of the German Awakening Movement roughly parallel with the Second Great Awakening in the early 1800s in American church history. The group of immigrants, from Saxony to Missouri in 1839, was very aware of being "awakened" and often described others as awakened, comparable to born again. The pastor who took leadership, Carl F. W. Walther, was Pietistic in instinct, although very conscious of pietistic excesses. In a small group of university students, he experienced such a relentless pursuit of sins to be repented that he went into a depression for a while. After reaching America, the first leader of the colony, their bishop, became embroiled in sexual sins and was banished. His departure caused great confusion about their identity as a church, which drove Walther again into a depression. He came out of it with a belief in ministry flowing from the priesthood of all believers, still uncharacteristic among Lutheran church bodies. Walther had had a personal awakening experience.

I personally experienced the tail end of this Pietist culture, with its prohibitions on dancing, gambling, and going to movies. We could not have dances at Lutheran high school, and a lot of band members once got into serious trouble for playing poker in the back of the bus on a trip. My oldest brother takes credit for persuading our parents that going to movies was okay. In retrospect, my other brother and I did not appreciate enough how fortunate we were that we could take our dime to either of two movie theaters, just blocks away, even on Sunday afternoons.

Most immigrants from Norway, the second largest source of Lutherans in America, came from churches heavily influenced by Lutheran Pietist leader Hans Nielsen Hauge, active around 1800. Lay preacher Elling Eielsen, the most prominent leader of the Haugean Movement in America, arrived in 1839, about the same time as Walther and company.

Lest these German and Norwegian movements seem obscure to Americans from other heritages, I highlight that the Christians shaped by these movements worked together to put their faith into action by founding and supporting hospitals, orphanages, and "old folks" homes. These movements are memorialized today in the many hospitals named Lutheran in urban centers of the Midwest, although any religious significance has by now been long displaced by government funding. According to some counts, Lutheran Social Service agencies are today the second largest non-governmental social service network in this country. Service was the distinguishing spiritual discipline of those Lutherans.

The purpose of these paragraphs on a slice of Protestant church history is to highlight the value of heartfelt convictions that came from characteristic Pietist emphasis on faith ignited by the Holy Spirit. Those Pietists recognized his light that gets brighter and that brings continuing growth in the righteousness of Christ. With the big journey from the old country in living memory, they could appreciate Christian living as an ongoing journey.

The dominant Lutheran leader of the eighteenth-century immigrants on the East Coast, Henry M. Muhlenberg, came to the new country from the Pietist center at the University of Halle, which was founded by Philip Spener forty years earlier. He spent considerable time sorting out good ministers for burgeoning Lutheran congregations.

Muhlenberg's lead request was, "Tell me about your second awakening." In other words, are you really a Christian, and what experience would lead you into the ministry? When did your convictions become heartfelt? Especially striking is the expectation that there should be a second awakening and perhaps a few more. That question ought to be restored in a new church culture revolving around Holy Spirit and grace. Anticipating several awakenings is better than focusing so much attention on a one-time conversion.

LAW AND GOSPEL

In his preparation to teach the book of Romans, Martin Luther had the breakthrough insight that later launched the Reformation. He was considering the phrase "righteousness of God" in Romans 3:21, 22. In the Latin and German, the relationship between "righteousness" and "God" is grammatically a genitive ending that is usually translated as God's righteousness. When Luther thought of a righteous God, he saw a God angry with his own sinful unrighteousness.

But that genitive can also be translated "from God." It finally dawned on him that this was righteousness *from* God, who attributed it to him 100 percent by grace. Luther realized that he was now positionally holy, by virtue of his being called by God, who had come to him as far back as his baptism. He was saved by grace alone, through faith alone. He had discovered proclaimed holiness. This turned out to be a fundamental change in worldview that changed the Western world.

The nineteenth-century German *Erweckungsbewegung* (Awakening Movement) brought a renewed interest in Martin Luther, from whom attention had slipped during the previous half century, now known as the Age of Enlightenment.

Carl F. W. Walther as scholarly young man immersed himself in the renewed study of Luther. He is widely recognized as the leading Lutheran churchman of nineteenth-century America. His lasting contribution is a set of informal lectures/discussions he had with seminary students, gathered around his desk on Friday evenings. As with Luther's Table Talks, students took notes, which were published and translated as *The Proper Distinction between Law and Gospel*, abridged in a current publication titled *God's No and God's Yes*.[79]

The wisest sequence is Law first, by preaching God's demands that brings repentance. Then comes the gospel announcement of forgiveness by grace through faith, which can produce heartfelt motivation to live God-pleasing lives. The constant hazard is to place so much emphasis on sanctified living that the freedom of justification by grace is diminished. Hence, the sequence is Law, followed by Gospel.

The opposite sequence of Gospel and then Law—grace followed by right behavior—is characteristic of John Calvin's theology. Being in the union with Christ that yields Christlike living is a bedrock Reformed conviction. This makes all the more striking the Reformed theologian Lewis Smedes's demonstration, laid out in this book in chapter 4, that in Paul's theology, Christlikeness and work of the Holy Spirit are two sides of the same coin. The coin is Father's relationship with us through the saving work of his Son on one side, and on the other side through the ongoing work today of the Holy Spirit, whom the Father and Son send.

When we focus on becoming more like Christ, we can too easily see this as human effort to be pursued by greater human diligence. In contrast, when we expect more godly living to flow from the heart work of the Holy Spirit, we are forced to recognize our ongoing sinfulness. Then, we are drawn to look to God as the source and power for living out more and more of the abundant life Christ promises.

Martin Luther, in the same commentary on Paul's letter to the Romans that had such an impact on young John Wesley about two hundred years later, noted the phrase, "God's grace and the gift that came by it," in Romans 5:15. Luther comments: "The words *grace* and *gift* differ in that *grace* actually means the faithfulness or favor that God bears toward us by his own choice, by which he is disposed to give us Christ and to pour into us the Holy Spirit with the *gifts* of the Spirit. The gifts and the Spirit grow in us daily but are not perfect." On Romans 8:1, he wrote, "God is so favorable and gracious to us that our sins are not regarded and not judged. Rather, God relates to us according to our faith in Christ until sin is killed."

In chapter 3, I referred to the gifts of the Spirit (*charismata*—grace gifts received) as Paul's second great teaching on grace. Unfortunately, it was overlooked in later centuries.

On those who think they are moved by their own human powers to say, "I believe," Luther comments that "since it is a human construction and idea that does not reach the depths of the heart, it does nothing, and no improvement of life follows. Faith is a work of God in us that changes us and makes us to be born anew."[80]

EVANGELICAL VS. LEGALISTIC CHURCH PRACTICES

There is one more lasting contribution from a Lutheran with Pietist roots. It comes from Pastor Heinrich C. Schwan, who carefully distinguished between church practices orientated to grace and the legalism seen in so many evangelical churches of his time, in the late nineteenth century. He was constantly on guard lest legalism slip into church life. Here are some of his observations:

✓   Since we expect justification before God, with renewal of the heart and the fruits of the Spirit only through the Gospel, in everything we do, we should have this one thing in mind to give free course and sway to the Gospel.

✓ Evangelical practice demands manifestation of faith and love but does not issue commands about their aim, amount, and mode.

✓ Evangelical practice does not make the state of grace dependent on keeping the Law.

✓ Evangelical practice bears with all manner of defects, imperfections, and sins, rather than to remove them merely in an external manner.

✓ Evangelical practice should flow from evangelical knowledge but does so rather seldom and slowly.

✓ Evangelical practice lets love be the queen of all commandments.[81]

A CHURCH CULTURE SUPPORTING OPENNESS TO THE SPIRIT

The intent of this essay is to distinguish the basic dynamics of life in Christ that can guide the formal organization of a congregation, to identify and support the purposes that a congregational partnership should pursue in their life together. What kind of church culture should a congregation strive to develop today?

Nineteenth-century German culture is a long way from the twenty-first–century American culture we live in now. That former culture was male dominated and status conscious in a way that allowed little room for the ministry-by-all that flows from recognition of the priesthood of all believers as the source for ministry. It was controlling in a way that left little room for the unpredictable flow of the Holy Spirit in affairs of the church. It was much more oriented to duty than to joy and love. It relied excessively on the motivation of guilt.

But the basic theology of the Pietists still makes a lot of sense today. Leaving those former cultural limitations behind, the question at hand is how to express those understandings of God, Christ, Holy Spirit, and gifts of the Spirit in a church culture that best exemplifies openness to growth in grace and the Spirit.

The answers to this question are what I have tried to offer in the eight chapters of *Your Encounters with the Holy Spirit*.

ENDNOTES

1. J. Harold Ellens, *Understanding Religious Experiences: What the Bible Says about Spirituality* (Praeger, 2008), 98.

2. T. M. Luhrmann, *When God Talks Back: Understanding the American Evangelical Relationship with God* (Knopf, 2012), xix, xxi.

3. Luhrmann, pp. 132-133.

4. Luhrmann, p. xx.

5. Robert D. Putnam, *Bowling Alone: The Collapse and Revival of American Community* (Simon and Schuster, 2000).

6. Diana Butler Bass, *Christianity After Religion: The End of Church and the Birth of a New Spiritual Awakening* (Harper One, 2012), 120.

7. Matthew A. Elliott, *Faithful Feelings: Rethinking Emotion in the New Testament* (Kregel, 2006), 18-52.

8. Gerald R. McDermott, *Seeing God: Twelve Reliable Signs of True Spirituality* (Intervarsity Press, 1995), 31,32.

9. William James, "Lecture III The Reality of the Unseen," *Varieties of Religious Experience: A Study in Human Nature 1902*, A Public Domain Book.

10. Ralph W. Hood, "The Facilitation of Religious Experience," in *Handbook of Religious Experience*, ed. Ralph W. Hood (Religious Education Press, 1995), 577.

11. H. Newton Malony, *Psychology of Religion: Personalities, Problems, Possibilities*, ed by H. Newton Malony (Baker, 1991), 203. Another helpful text is *Psychology and Religion: Classic and Contemporary Views*, by Davd M. Wulff, (John Wiley, 1991).

12. "The Smalcald Articles" Part III, Article IV, in the *Book of Concord: The Confessions of the Evangelical Lutheran Church*, trans. and ed. by Theodore G. Tappert (Concordia Publishing House, 1959), 310.

13. J. T. Richardson, "The active vs passive convert: Paradigm conflict in conversion/recruitment research." *Journal for the Scientific Study of Religion*. 1985, pp. 166-172., as found in Ralph W. Hood, Bernard Spilka, Bruce Humsberger, Richard Gorsuch, *The Psychology of Religion: An Empirical Approach*, 2nd Edition (Guildor Press, 1996), 283.

14. J. Harold Ellens, *Understanding Religious Experiences* (Praeger, 2008), 94.

15. David S. Luecke, *Talking With God: How Ordinary Christians Grow in Prayer* (Fellowship Ministries, 1997), 59, 60.

16. David S. Luecke and Samuel Southard, *Pastoral Administration: Integrating Ministry and Management in the Church* (Word Books, 1986).

17. Scott Thumma and Warren Bird, "Changes in American Megachurches: Tracing Eight Years of Growth and Innovation in the Nation's Largest-attendance Congregations," (Hartford Institute for Religion Research), 2008. (http://hirr.hartsem.edu/megachurch/megastoday2008_summaryreport.html).

18. *Smalcald Articles*, Part III, Article IV.

19. Acts 4: 31; 6: 3, 5, 8; 11:24.

20. Karl Rahner, *The Spirit in the Church* (Seabury Press, 1979), 21.

21. Brian Kolodiejchuk, *Mother Teresa: Come By My Light: The Private Writings of the Saint of Calcutta* (Crown Publishing, 2007).

22. Bill Hybels, The *Power of a Whisper: Hearing God and Having the Guts to Respond* (Zondervan, 2010), 43-44.

23. Dallas Willard, *Hearing God: Developing a Conversational Relationship with God* (Inter Varsity Press, 1999), 170.

24. Gerald R. McDermott, *Seeing God: Twelve Reliable Signs of True Spirituality* (Intervarsity Press, 1995), 32-41.

25. Grant McClug, "Pentecostals: the Sequel," *Christianity Today* (April 1, 2006).

26. Donald E. Miller and Tetsunao Yamamori, *Global Pentecostalism: The New Face of Christian Social Engagement* (University of California Press, 2007), 26-28.

27. From Lewis Smedes, *Union with Christ* (Eerdmans, 1989), 43, 44.

   "The same oneness of Christ and Spirit is found everywhere. Notice this series of parallels:

   We are sealed in Christ (Eph. 1:13)
   We are sealed in the Spirit (Eph. 1:13)
   We are consecrated in Christ (I Cor. 1: 2.)
   We are consecrated in the Holy Spirit (Rom. 15: 15).
   We are righteous in Christ (Phil. 3:8-9).
   We are righteous in the Holy Spirit (Rom. 14: 17).
   We are righteous in both (1 Cor. 6:11).
   We have life through Christ (Eph. 2:1; Col. 3: 4).
   We have life through the Holy Spirit (Rom. 8: 11).
   We have hope grounded in Christ (1 Cor. 15:9).
   We have hope grounded in the power of the Spirit (Rom. 5:5; Gal. 6:8).
   Christ is the alternative to the law of sin and death (Rom. 10:4).
   The Spirit is the alternative to the law of sin and death (Rom. 8:2).
   The following suggest a more dynamic picture; they press for action:
   We are commanded to stand fast in the Lord (Phil. 4:1).
   We are told to stand fast in the one Spirit (Phil. 4:4).
   We are told to rejoice in the Lord (Phil. 4:4).
   We are told to have joy in the Holy Spirit (Rom. 14:17).
   We are told to live in Christ (Col. 2:6).
   We are told to walk in the Spirit (Eph. 4: 3; Gal. 5: 25).
   Paul speaks the truth in the Christ (Rom. 9:11; 2 Cor. 2: 17).
   Paul speaks the truth in the Spirit (1 Cor. 12: 3).
   We are called into the fellowship of Christ (1 Cor. 1: 9).
   We are blessed with the fellowship of the Holy Spirit (Cor. 13:14)."

28. Charles J. Keating, *Who We Are Is How We Pray* (Twenty-Third Publications, 1987).

29. Gary Thomas, *Sacred Pathways: Discover Your Soul's Path to God* (Zondervan, 2000), 215.

30. Scott Thumma and Warren Bird, "Changes in American Megachurches: Tracing Eight Years of Growth and Innovation in the Nation's Largest-attendance Congregations" (Hartford Institute for Religion Research, 2008. http://hirr.hartsem.edu/megachurch/megastoday2008_summaryreport.html).

31. Jonathan Edwards, "Personal Narrative," in Jonathan Edwards, *Basic Writings*, ed. Ola Winslow (Penguin, 1966), 87.

32. Eugene H. Peterson, *Under the Unpredictable Plant*,(Eerdmans, 1992), 134.

33. Robert Fuller, *Spiritual but Not Religious: Understanding Unchurched America* (Oxford, 2001), as quoted in Diane Butler Bass, *Christianity after Religion* (HarperOne, 2012), 67.

[34] Diane Butler Bass, *Christianity after Religion: The End of Church and the Birth of a New Spiritual Awakening* (Harper One, 2012).

Andrew Farley, *God without Religion: Can it Really Be This Simple?* (Baker Books, 2011).

Rick James, *Jesus without Religion*, (IVP Books, 2007).

[35] J. Harold Ellens, *Understandng Religious Experiences* (Praeger, 2008), 98.

[36] Ellens, 95.

[37] James W. Jones, *The Spirit and the World* (Hawthorn, 1975), 33, 41, 44.

[38] C. F. W. Walther, "We are No Longer What We Were," in *Selected Sermons of C.F.W. Walther*, tr. Henry Eggold (Concordia Publishing House, 1981), 155-163.

[39] Greg L. Hawkins, Cally Parkinson, *Reveal* (Willow Creek Resources, 2007)

[40] Janet O. Hagbert and Robert A. Guelich, *The Critical Journey: Stages in the Life of Faith*, (Word Publishing, 1989), 10.

[41] James W. Fowler. *Stages of Faith: The Psychology of Human Development and the Quest for Meaning* (Harper One, 1995).

[42] Thomas A. Droege, *Faith Passages and Patterns* (Fortress Press, 1983), 77-81.

[43] James E. Loder, *The Transforming Moment,* second ed. (Helmers and Howard, 1989), 10.

[44] Gordon D. Fee, "On Getting the Spirit Back into Spirituality," in *Life in the Spirit*, ed. Jeffrey Greenman and George Kalantzis (IVP, 2010), 43.

[45] Loder, *Transforming Moment*, 19.

[46] Loder, *Transforming Moment*, 22-24.

[47] John Shea, *An Experience Named Spirit* (Thomas More Press, 1983), 12.

[48] Shea, 98.

[49] Leonard Sweet, *Post Modern Pilgrims* (Broadman andHolman,2000).

[50] Shea, 95.

[51] Shea, 104.

[52] Shea, 101.

[53] Shea 35.

[54] Shea, 49.

[55] Shea, 46.

[56] Shea, 87.

[57] Shea, 54.

[58] Ralph W. Hook, Bernard Spilka, Bruce Humsberger, Richard Gorsuch, *The Psychology of Religion: An Empirical Approach*, 2nd Edition (Guildor Press, 1996), 283.

[59] Greg L Hawkins and Cally Parkinson, *Move: What 1,000 Churches REVEAL about Spiritual Growth* (Zondervan, 2011), 266.

[60] Christian A. Schwarz, *Natural Church Development: A Guide to Eight Essential Qualities of Healthy Churches* (Church Smart, 1998), 22-37.

[61] Max Lucado, *Come Thirsty*, (W Publishing Group, 2004), 60.

[62] Loren E. Halverson, "Prayer and Action," in *A Primer on Prayer*, ed. by Paul R. Sponheim, (Fortress, 1988), 98.

[63] Rebecca Button Prichard, "Do Miracles Still Happen?," *Presbyterians Today*, (March 1999).

[64] Bengt Hoffman, *Luther and the Mystics* (Augsburg, 1976), 195-200.

[65] Ken Blue, *Authority to Heal* (IVP, 1987) 43.

66. Rober Wuthnow, *After Heaven: Spirituality in America Since the 1950s* (University of California Press, 1998), 122.

67. Keener, *Miracles: The Credibility of the New Testament Accounts* (Baker Academic, 2011), 201, 203.

68. Paul Prather, *Modern-Day Miracles: How Ordinary People Experience Supernatural Acts of God* (Andres and McMeel, 1996), 66.

69. Christian A. Schwarz, *Natural Church Development: A Guide to Eight Essential Qualities of Healthy Churches*, 3rd edition (Church Smart Resources, 1998), 31.

70. Edgar H. Schein, *Organizational Culture and Leadership*, 4th edition (Jossey Bass, 2010), 29.

71. Schein, 25

72. Samuel R. Chand, *Cracking Your Church's Culture* (Jossey Bass, 2011), 1.

73. Schein, 29.

74. Johann Arndt, *True Christianity* translated by Peter Erb, from *Classics of Western Spirituality* (Paulist Press, 1979), 184.

75. C. John Weborg, "Reborn in Order to Renew," in *Christian History* (Volume 5, Number 2), 17-18, 34-35.

76. C. John Weborg, 34.

77. Everett F. Harrison, "Holiness," *The International Standard Bible Encyclopedia*, ed. by Geoffrey W. Bromily, Vol 2, (Eerdmans Publishing, 1982), 728.

78. F. E. Mayer, *The Religious Bodies of America* (Concordia Publishing House, 1961), 306.

79. C. F. W. Walther, *God's No and God's Yes*, (CPH, 1973).

80. From the "Preface to the Epistle to the Romans:," *Luther's Spirituality*, ed and trans by Philip and Peter Krey (Paulist Press, 2007), 108,109.

81. Heinrich C. Schwan, "Propositions on Unevangelical Practice," in *Concordia Theological Monthly*, (May 1945), 288-294.

CPSIA information can be obtained at www.ICGtesting.com
Printed in the USA
LVOW11s1217211214

419607LV00006B/3/P